What Does It Mean to Be a Christian?

Other Books of Interest from St. Augustine's Press

Dietrich von Hildebrand, *The Nature of Love*

Kenneth D. Whitehead (editor), *The Church, Marriage, & the Family*

Alain Besançon, *Protestant Nation*

Wayne J. Hankey, *Aquinas's Neoplatonism in the Summa Theologiae on God: A Short Introduction*

Kenneth Baker, S.J., *The Mystery of Death and Beyond*

Glenn Arbery (editor), *So Ancient and So New: St. Augustine's Confessions and Its Influence*

Gary M. Bouchard, *Southwell's Sphere: The Influence of England's Secret Poet*

Étienne Gilson, *Theology and the Cartesian Doctrine of Freedom*

James V. Schall, *The Praise of 'Sons of Bitches': On the Worship of God by Fallen Men*

James V. Schall, *The Regensburg Lecture*

Charles Cardinal Journet, *The Mass: The Presence of the Sacrifice of the Cross*

Gerard V. Bradley, *Unquiet American: U.S. Catholics and America's Common Good*

Edward Feser, *The Last Superstition: A Refutation of the New Atheism*

Ernest A. Fortin, A.A., *Christianity and Philosophical Culture in the Fifth Century: The Controversy about the Human Soul in the West*

Peter Kreeft, *Ecumenical Jihad*

Peter Kreeft, *Socrates' Children: The 100 Greatest Philosophers*

Josef Pieper, *The Christian Idea of Man*

Josef Pieper and Heinz Raskop, *What Catholics Believe*

Karl Rahner, *Encounters with Silence*

Roger Scruton, *An Intelligent Person's Guide to Modern Culture*

Roger Kimball, *The Fortunes of Permanence: Culture and Anarchy in an Age of Amnesia*

Frederic Raphael and Joseph Epstein, *Where Were We?*

What Does It Mean to Be a Christian?

A Debate

John F. Crosby and Stafford Betty

ST. AUGUSTINE'S PRESS
South Bend, Indiana

Manufactured in the United States of America.

1 2 3 4 5 6   25 24 23 22 21 20 19

Library of Congress Cataloging in Publication Data
Names: Crosby, John F., 1944- author.
Title: What does it mean to be a Christian? : a debate between orthodoxy and new age theology / John F. Crosby and Stafford Betty.
Description: 1st [edition].
South Bend, Indiana : St. Augustines Press, Inc., 2016.
Includes index.
Identifiers: LCCN 2016033735
ISBN 9781587319365 (paperbound : alk. paper)
Subjects: LCSH: Christianity and other religions--New Age movement.
New Age movement--Relations--Christianity.
Classification: LCC BR128.N48 C76 2016
DDC 261.2--dc23 LC record available at https://lccn.loc.gov/2016033735

∞ The paper used in this publication meets the minimum
requirements of the American National Standard for Information Sciences -
Permanence of Paper for Printed Materials, ANSI Z39.48-1984.

St. Augustine's Press
www.staugustine.net

John's Introduction

Stafford Betty and John F. Crosby grew up together in Mobile, Alabama. We were good friends already as teens, and our friendship grew as our faith grew. We were deeply united in our shared Catholic faith, and in fact this was the strongest bond between us. But then there came a certain parting of the ways in our early twenties. Just at the time when John encountered the person and the work of Dietrich von Hildebrand, and also immersed himself in the work of John Henry Newman, Stafford began his graduate theology studies at Fordham University. John was drawn by von Hildebrand and Newman to go deeper in his Catholic faith and to take it more seriously than he had ever taken it before, whereas Stafford, who lost his faith following a year in Vietnam as a lieutenant in the Army Corps of Engineers, had an encounter with Hindu and Buddhist thought at Fordham that led to a new kind of faith. No longer able to accept the Christian claim that Jesus Christ as the God-man gives the definitive revelation of the Father and effects the one and only real reconciliation of God and man, Stafford came to think that other world religions offered as reliable a path of salvation as Christianity. At the time when Newman was becoming for John the norm of his Catholic belief, the pluralist theologians John Hick and Huston Smith were becoming for Stafford the guiding lights behind his post-Christian theism. Thus did we two friends diverge almost half a century ago, and thus do we diverge to this day.

Over the years we have often discussed and debated the matters of faith that divide us. (We have also discussed matters that still unite us, such as the rejection of eliminative materialism and of atheism.) But in 2009 our exchange took a somewhat different direction. John had the idea of discussing not whose religious position was the right one, but whose position could count as the Christian one. Could Stafford still call himself Christian even while thinking that Christianity is no more based on a special revelatory initiative of God than Hinduism? Of course, we were not entirely able to prescind from our own strong beliefs. When John, for example, would present what he takes to be the distinctively Christian position, he could hardly avoid implying that this was much the more reasonable position. The same for Stafford speaking to John. And yet, our exchange was different from the debates of earlier days; we were trying to understand each other and to explain ourselves to each other, and not just to refute each other. This is why our exchange ran on for almost two years, and why we both felt it to be a particularly fruitful exchange. So fruitful as to be of interest to other religiously concerned persons.

John F. Crosby

Stafford's Introduction

This book records a conversation between two philosopher-theologians with different ways of conceiving God and practicing Christianity. One of the speakers is John F. Crosby, a personalist philosopher teaching at staunchly Catholic Franciscan University in Steubenville, Ohio. The other is Stafford Betty, a "New Thought" philosopher teaching at staunchly secular California State University in Bakersfield. Both are believers. Both think of God as personal, not some impersonal force out of Star Wars. Both are prayerful men.

So what, you might ask, can they disagree on to such a point that it takes a book to bring it all out? It won't take long to discover two very different ways of being in the world—one of them instinctively conservative and protective of a long and great tradition, the Catholic faith that defined and nurtured him from boyhood on; the other, though equally nurtured by that same faith, always ready to look for something he took to be more plausible. In his many publications John tries to penetrate ever more deeply the mystery of what it means to be a person. His primary subject is his own inner experience as seen through the lens of Catholic teaching—from Aquinas to Newman to his mentor Dietrich von Hildebrand. Stafford has spent much of his career looking outward at the world's major religions, especially Asian, and has watered his garden with the insights of thinkers like Emerson and Tolstoy, and more recent pluralist theologians like John Hick, Huston Smith, Diana Eck, and Marcus Borg.

John is intent on defending the uniqueness and superiority of the Christian God and of Catholic Christianity. His commitment to the Bible as a special revelation from God and of the Church's ecumenical councils as reliable amplifications of that revelation is unwavering. Stafford interprets the world through the spiritual, mystical, and psychic experiences of men and women from several of the world's great faiths. For him God's presence resonates in the soul's deepest core; no special revelation from outside is necessary. In many other ways John and Stafford butt heads, but they are united in their personalism. The reader will no doubt be surprised to discover that theism can be packaged so differently.

Is one packaged better than the other? Is one more likely than the other to approximate the way God really is? Is much riding on the choice you make? John thinks it matters greatly, while Stafford thinks it matters less. John thinks that Stafford has made serious mistakes with serious conse- quences that affect the way one prays and views the sacraments, while Stafford thinks that John's conclusions owe too much to Church teaching and lack plausibility in the modern age. Readers will find much to ponder in their many skirmishes, always delivered with respect and often outward signs of an old friendship, reaching all the way back to boyhood, that has weathered half a century.

Stafford Betty

The Letters

January 30, 2010
Dear Stafford,

Many thanks for your last message, with the photos and your article, "Hinduism, the cousinly religion of Catholicism." You look so distinguished in the photos with the Hindu swamis—the very picture of a wise man.

The points of contact between Hinduism and Catholicism that you discuss are very interesting. And I can understand that, from your point of view, Hindus and Christians just give different names, as you say, to the same divine realities, and are two equally efficacious instruments of salvation. But what I can't understand is how you can think that a committed Christian can believe in this equivalence. It is not a question of pre- and post-Vatican II; it is simply a question of what Christianity fundamentally and inalienably is. There is a sense in which you seem to me, and have long seemed to me, not to let Christians be Christians. I would be in a much better position to learn from you about Hinduism if you were not constantly, as it seems to me, blurring certain basic boundaries. We have talked about this many times.

My best to Monica. As always I am eager to have news of Louie.

A blessing on your weekend, Stafford.
John

*   *   *   *   *   *   *   *   *   *   *   *

January 31, 2010
Dear John,

Good to hear from you, as always.

I have been worrying about what you say more acutely than usual. Perhaps it is counter-productive to look for common denominators in the major world religions. But if we don't—and this is my defense—then we are left with Christians being Christians and Hindus being Hindus and Muslims being Muslims and Jews being Jews. Doesn't that sound like a recipe for disaster?

Using that approach it would follow that, in the realm of politics, it's advisable to just let Democrats be Democrats and Republicans be Republicans. But is that really the way to make progress? We know it's not.

So I hope that we can see common themes in the major world religions in the hope that we'll respect each other more and get along better with each other. I certainly don't think that demythologizing the various stories or theologies so precious to religion is their most important task of the moment, but it isn't an insignificant one.

The religion of the future that I envisage for our shrinking planet will appreciate all these stories and place them side by side, the Gita being read next to the Gospels on Sunday morning. At some point I hope we'll give up on the idea of special revelation top-down and view religion as man's attempt to build a relation with the Divine from the bottom up. Fortunately it does appear that there are eruptions of divine light in the best of us, but these eruptions always occur within a particular cultural context, and thus none of the world's sages or saints can be trusted to have the last word on how best to relate to or conceptualize God or the divine world.

Sometimes I wish it were easier to see the Big Picture ready-made, but on the other hand I enjoy the process of gradually seeing more and more of it as the years roll by. I think that's the way God, Deus Absconditus, intended it.

Blessings,
Stafford

*   *   *   *   *   *   *   *   *   *   *   *

February 7, 2010
Dear Stafford,

Many thanks for listening to me and responding thoughtfully. I was struck by this in your message: we have to get away from "the idea of special revelation top-down and view religion as man's attempt to build a relation with the Divine from the bottom up." I am puzzled as to why a religious person like you would set aside the first way so resolutely and take the second way as the only legitimate form of religion. Perhaps you remember how Simmias in the Phaedo says that we have no choice but to trust frail philosophical arguments *unless a divine word should come to us and give us more clarity than we can get on our own.* How can a religious person not long to hear such a divine word? If God is personal and if religion is interpersonal, how can we fail to suffer under the situation of not hearing a divine word addressed to us? In any case, and this is my second reaction to your statement, the idea of God taking the initiative and revealing Himself to us is constitutive of Christianity. Whoever talks to Christians as if they should think of their religion as just another human attempt, from the bottom up, to imagine God, does not understand who he is talking to. He is trying to bend Christians into a shape that is not their own. What I wanted to say in my last message is that you have often seemed to me like this person.

We were inundated last night with almost two feet of snow, then this afternoon the sky cleared and became radiantly blue. The snow-covered world in this afternoon light was beautiful to behold.

I just finished a study of Newman and I can't tell whether it would interest you. I'm attaching it just in case, but feel free to ignore it if it doesn't fit in with your current interests.

A blessing on you and Monica,
John

*   *   *   *   *   *   *   *   *   *   *

Feb. 13, 2010
Dear John,

Thanks for your challenging commentary. It's brought on some deep thinking, which I will try to put into words.

I have a profound, hopefully unshakable faith that we as individuals are loved by God, even if that means He does not know us and address us by name—not yet, not at our humble level. I hope He does, but I am not sure. It seems just as likely that his holy spirit—his grace, his creative energy, whatever you want to call it—is embedded within us and is the substance of our very souls, our very selves, and that we pray best when we meditate on and sink into and live out of that holy depth. This, incidentally, is a very Hindu notion straight out of the Upanishads. It appeals to me in part, perhaps even mainly, because I have experienced so little answer to my prayers over the years and decades. That personal relationship you speak of, in which one listens to the other and helps that other, does not square with my actual experience.

For philosophical reasons I believe, however, that God is personal, indeed the Supreme Person. It stands to reason that the Creator would create beings as much like Himself as possible—finite versions of what He is. So I have no trouble with the notion of personhood. I just don't see with any clarity that God meets me in quite the way you imagine, as much as I might like Him to.

For me it is enough that I have access to the techniques of meditation, and I do. I can know God as deeply as I want to. There is a sense in which my prayers are addressed to my own depths, for that is where God meets me. The point of the spiritual life is to divinize ourselves as much as possible, and the effort is wonderfully worthwhile.

I would describe this effort as a bottom-up approach, even though God's creation of us all was obviously top-down. My faith tells me that God expects us to make a great effort to liberate that little slice of potential divinity that we are, and that if this process were easy it wouldn't be worth doing. It *would* be too easy if God answered our prayers in the way we might, in our weakness and ignorance, think He should—to be specific, in the way we might have wished Him to interfere in the healing of your sister Jane, or the release of my mother from her decrepit old body when she wishes so ardently to go home to Him. Once done, once we have surrenderd our will to his and ennobled ourselves in the way He wants us to, we have added to the value of the universe, and that is what He wants all of us to do.

As regards Christianity, I think the Christian experiences grace and salvation through the example of Jesus, an extraordinary man whose divine depths were unusually transparent to him. He, and many like him in the course of the world's spiritual history, have shown us what is possible. It might even seem that God has descended into flesh, perhaps many times (as in the Hindu avatar doctrine), in some kind of supernatural eruption. This may be the case—I can't say it isn't—but it's easier for me to believe that the process of mankind's sanctification requires no such eruption. We have the ability by virtue of the divine sliver within us, what you and I would call the spiritual soul, what Hindus call the Atman, what Buddhists call Buddha Nature, to sanctify ourselves without so unnatural an eruption. It is true that I am trying to bend Christians into a shape that is not their own. If a person comes across a better shape, he owes it to the people he loves to introduce them to it. Maybe it will fit better if given a chance.

Stafford

* * * * * * * * * * * *

Feb 21, 2010
Dear Stafford,

Let me pick up with your last comment, which refers back to my previous email. It is quite in order to try to bend your friends into a new shape when you think you have found a new one; my concern is with calling the new shape Christian when it is in fact fundamentally opposed to the Christian idea. The name "Christian" has a certain prestige among you and your interlocutors and it is a rhetorical advantage with these interlocutors to call your position Christian; but you may have to forego this advantage for the sake of calling things by their proper names. The bottom-up approach to religion cannot, it seems to me, be harmonized with a religion in which God takes the initiative towards us men.

Your latest message confirms me in my sense of this divergence from Christianity. For you say that you can come to know God as deeply as you want, simply by using techniques of meditation. You approach God, He doesn't approach you. You control the relation and degree of contact, He does not confound your techniques and break in on you.

You speak of us human beings "sanctifying ourselves" and "ennobling ourselves." When you mention "grace," making me think at first that here at least you recognize not just self-sanctification but God sanctifying us, you dash my hope by identifying grace with "the substance of our very souls," so that in the end the action of grace is just me sanctifying myself. What you call sanctification seems to me to be a kind of spiritual athleticism and not Christian sanctification. In Christian terms, you represent the extremest Pelagianism. Just the other day I was looking with my students at this passage in Rudolf Otto, who, speaking about grace as it is known in Christian experience, says:

The idea of 'election'—i.e. of having been chosen out and pre-ordained by God *unto salvation*—is an immediate and pure expression of the actual religious experience of grace. The recipient of divine grace feels and knows ever more and more surely, as he looks back on his past, that he has not grown into his present self through any achievement or effort of his own, and that, apart from his own will or power, grace was imparted to him, grasped him, impelled, and led him. And even the resolves and decisions that were most his own and most free become to him, without losing the element of freedom, something that he *experienced* rather than *did*. Before every deed of his own he sees love the deliverer in action, seeking and selecting, and acknowledges that an eternal gracious purpose is watching over his life (*The Idea of the Holy*, 87).

Nothing here of your predominant focus on self-sanctification. Otto expresses well the Christian experience of God working in us, and what he says is as far as could be from your idea that we, using techniques of meditation, are in control of our union with God.

In my message of December 22 I raised some points I'd like to get your reaction to.

I was in Tampa this weekend, having been invited to speak to our Board of Trustees about a reform of the core curriculum, something I've fought for for years. I think you and I would be on the same side of that battle.

I'm still looking for word of Louie.

In friendship,
John

*　*　*　*　*　*　*　*　*　*　*

February 27, 2010
Dear John,

I have read your latest sally with great interest and delight. I'll be responding to the third paragraph below.

Let's begin with Pelagianism. Wikipedia accurately describes it this way: "It is the belief that original sin did not taint human nature and that mortal will is still capable of choosing good or evil without special Divine aid. Thus, Adam's sin was 'to set a bad example' for his progeny, but his actions did not have the other consequences imputed to Original Sin. . . . In short, humanity has full control, and thus full responsibility, for obeying the Gospel *in addition to* full responsibility for every sin (the latter insisted upon by both proponents and opponents of Pelagianism)."

You are roughly correct to describe me as a Pelagian, though of course I do not believe that Adam was a real man or that "original sin" contaminated future generations in the way a traditionalist would have it. With that out of the way, let me get to the meat of your critique.

I do believe in self-sanctification, but not quite in the way you suppose. God's grace, or energy, or saving power, or sheer *presence,* is always within us. He doesn't choose one person over another, as Calvin taught, or turn his grace on and off for reasons we cannot fathom. His grace is like the water of a swimming pool. It is always there for us to dive into, and if we know how to swim just a little bit, it will always buoy us up. Once in the pool, it's up to us to swim. If we step out of the pool, it's up to us to dive in again. I grant you that the unfailing presence of God's grace implies that God has a steadfastness and a dependability that is unlike human persons. I suspect that this unlikeness has led you to believe that God is therefore *not personal* when conceived of in the way I've described. I would say that He is *perfectly* personal, and that anything short of this kind of perfection in the Godhead would make him too much like us, and therefore liable to the charge of being finite.

I read the quotation by Otto with interest, and I agree that he is accurately describing the Christian experience. But his analysis of the experience would not be mine. He writes, "The recipient of divine grace feels and knows ever more and more surely, as he looks back on his past, that he has not grown into his present self through any achievement or effort of his own, and that, apart from his own will or power, grace was imparted to him, grasped him, impelled, and led him." I would put it this way: "What feels like a descent of divine grace into our hearts from above is really the fruit of our own effort. When I sit in prayer, often I get nowhere. Why is this? Is it because God has decided not to visit me? No, it's because I have not made the necessary effort to meet Him. Perhaps I am too sleepy and should go back to bed. Or maybe I haven't removed the distractions that are blocking Him out: I don't really *want* to meet Him; instead I would rather be diverted. But if I make the effort, He is there—unfailingly." This is more than a hypothesis; it is the way I actually experience prayer (and less often, meditation). Do you really mean to say that it's *God's* fault that you have dry spells in your prayer life? Does God really decline to meet the sincere aspirant?

There is another problem with Otto. He writes, "And even the resolves and decisions that were most his own and most free become to him, without losing the element of freedom, something that he experienced rather than did." I would argue that if you don't *do* something, but instead it's done to you, you cannot be said to be free. How can you *not* lose the element of freedom if you are not even the doer? Otto sounds suprisingly like Calvin, whose doctrine of election makes God arbitrary, and therefore not God at all, or at least not the God I could love. It's not that I would mind being chosen; it's that others are not. I cannot take seriously a God who chooses some and rejects others, unless the choosing is based on something the creature freely undertakes. But you seem to be saying that's Pelagianism.

My sister Stephanie always gives God the credit for her good deeds and takes all the blame for her bad ones. That's no more logical than taking credit for her good deeds and blaming the devil for her bad ones. It seems to me we should take both the credit and the blame because we are equally the choosers in both cases.

I look forward to your response. I hope you will show me why you and Otto are far removed from Calvin and his predestinarianism. And, of course, I would be pleased if you could show me where I am wrong in my analysis.

Louie is in transition. Like most of the young men around him, he feels more at home in bars and night clubs than in churches. But there are always signs of light trying to break through; he sees, for example, the utter futility of materialism and is doing his dissertation on a French writer who shares this conviction, though unfortunately the same writer *is* a materialist! You can bet I lose sleep over Louie from time to time.

Wishing you every blessing, and good health to Pia,
Stafford

* * * * * * * * * * *

March 13, 2010
Dear Stafford,

Many thanks for your latest. Sorry to make you wait for an answer. That's in part my busyness, but also in part the need to mull over your thoughts and to do justice to them. We both want to avoid an exchange in which we just score "debater's points" against each other.

I had originally just meant to address the question of what is properly called Christian and what not, and I'd like not to lose track of that question as we proceed beyond it.

There is indeed a way of affirming God's grace and God's "election" to the point of obscuring the freedom of the creature, and you and I concur in rejecting the extreme predestinarian doctrines. But there is also a way of affirming the freedom of the creature to the point of obscuring the creatureliness of the creature and the sovereignty of God.

It is true that the Otto quote seems in one place to make us passive under the influence of divine grace, but in other places he tries to comprehend the interpenetration of human freedom and divine sovereignty, as when he says: "It is next to be noted that predestination in this sense, as identical with the absolute supremacy of the *numen*, has nothing whatever to do with the unfree will of Determinism. Rather, it finds very frequently precisely in the free will of the creature the contrast which makes it stand out so prominently. ... In the face of the eternal power man is reduced to naught, together with his free choice and action. And the eternal power waxes immeasurable just because it fulfils its decrees despite the freedom of human will."

Sometimes I get the impression that you think that God acts in your life only to the degree that you at your own initiative open yourself to Him. As I see it, and as Christians have always seen it, God isn't God, and God certainly isn't a personal God, if He is not again and again acting on His initiative, often surprising us, often overwhelming us. Aslan "is good but not tame," as C. S. Lewis says of this Christ-figure that he created in the *Chronicles of Narnia*," and he would be tame in a very un-godlike way if he always acted towards me only in response to my initiative. Your talk about self-sanctification seems to me to leave out the divine initiative, and as a result, contrary to your intention, to reduce our relation to God to something sub-personal. A real I-Thou encounter requires unpredictable initiatives on both sides.

As for the inner prayer in which we seek union with God, here too I would stress the divine initiative as distinct from my own initiative. Don't we find seasons of grace, moments of kairos, and also times of aridity in which the absence of God oppresses us? Do you really think that every moment that falls short of joyous union with God results from some deficiency on my side? I agree with you that these alternations never come from some lack in God's generosity, but I don't see that it follows that they come only from some lack in me; I see them instead as being often rooted in the dynamics of interpersonal encounter, and in a certain creativity that belongs to all such encounters.

What emerges from our exchange is a concern of mine that Christian existence involves an interpersonal relation to God that seems to me missing in your own conception of religion. By the way, you gave me further grounds for this concern when you wrote back in December that God cannot be present to everything in the universe, and loses track of developments on earth when He is occupied with other parts of the universe. I wrote back saying that it would seem to follow from your view that He cannot be present to all 7 billion human beings in a personal, individual way, since His attention to some would presumably interfere with His attention to others. This would mean that when you turn to Him in prayer, He may or may not be available to respond to you; that which you say is always there for you would then have to be something like a divine medium in which you bathe, but it would not necessarily be God encountering you person to person.

I look forward to hearing your responses, and to continuing our exchange as long as you think it is bearing fruit. Best wishes to Monica.

Yours in ancient friendship,
John

*   *   *   *   *   *   *   *   *   *   *

March 15, 2010
Dear John,

Please be assured I'm not interested in debating points either. I've really had to do some soul-searching to deal with your latest letter. I thank you for it.

I'm glad you clarified Otto's position. We can lay him to rest for the moment.

Do you know of Anthony Bloom? He is a "metropolitan" (or bishop) in the Russian Orthodox Church and writes insightfully on prayer. You would like what he says here:

> We must just come to God in order to be in his presence, and, if he chooses to make us aware of it, blessed be God, but if he chooses to make us experience his real absence, blessed be God again, because as we have seen he is free to come near or not. . . . Our sense of God's absence may be the result of his will; he may want us to long for him and to learn how precious his presence is by making us know by experience what utter loneliness means. But often our experience of God's absence is determined by the fact that we do not give ourselves a chance of becoming aware of his presence (*Living Prayer* 102-03).

I'm inclined to think that our experience of God's absence is *always* determined by "the fact that we do not give ourselves a chance of becoming aware of his presence." Yesterday in church, when the great parable of the Prodigal Son was read, what struck me was the delight of the father in the son's return. I imagine the father keeping a constant, never waning eye on the road leading to the estate. I imagine that God is similarly available to us. What you call the "divine initiative" and Bloom calls God's freedom "to come near or not" sounds all too human to me. It is hard enough preparing ourselves for coming into his presence without his making it even more difficult by not showing up! "A real I-Thou encounter requires unpredictable initiatives on both sides," you say. I would say that such an encounter requires an unpredictable initiative on only one side—ours. There will always be a certain unpredictability in our relationship with God, in this and any future world, because we always will be finite and less than completely steadfast. I ask myself, Does God become more interesting or attractive to me if He were to sometimes absent himself when I seek his presence? You might think this would happen if God's perfect dependability, his unfailing availability to us, led to our taking Him for granted. While it is true that big shots in our world sometimes make themselves more sought after by making themselves scarce, God would not need to resort to such a device, and it would be stingy if He did so. There are innumerable dimensions to his glory. As soon as we plumb one of them, we stumble across another. We could never grow tired of his glory because we could never get to the bottom of it.

What you require of God is that He have an intimate knowledge of and interest in you. You delighted in von Hildebrand's singular love for you when he was alive, and certainly we all love to be regarded as special in the eyes of the people we admire and seek approval from. God is Perfection; He is everything you could ever admire and want to be loved by, so of course you want to be known by Him. I, too, want to be known and loved by God. But I suspect that the relation between the Creator and creature is more intimate than you guess. You describe my view of Him as "a divine 'medium' in which you bathe." That is an apt description. It is the way that some of Christianity's mystics speak of God. This "medium" is what serious meditators, especially those Christians using centering prayer, seek to immerse themselves in. The only question remaining is whether this "medium" can be thought of as personal, and therefore Christian. First we need to drop that slightly disparaging term "medium." Let's use the term "Being" instead. Can this Being in which the mystic immerses himself be described as personal? I think so. The essence of personhood is awareness. And God is infinitely aware. He is aware of Himself and of us. The quality of that awareness completely transcends our language, but "loving" and "blissful" is not a bad place to start. When we immerse ourselves in this wonderful Being in our rare moments of focused prayer or meditation, we are relating to a unique kind of awareness, a unique kind of person, the Supreme Person. But does this Person *relate back to us?* If not, the relation would be onesided, unfulfilling, perhaps even devastating. *We want to be known and loved as the particular beings that we are.*

My study of and limited practice of centering prayer tells me that we are known in so intimate a way that the language of union is more appropriate than the language of I-Thou. Actually neither excludes the other. And neither is more Christian than the other, though it must be admitted that the language of union prevails more in the religions of India than in the West.

Of course, most Christians use the language of praise or petitionary prayer when relating to God, so the language of union would be alien to them and might seem impersonal. I too use petitionary prayer. But I don't think it's more *personal* than centering prayer.

The God we meet when we successfully center ourselves is, I think, always present for us. We encounter God within us, not outside. "Find the door of the inner chamber of your soul and you will discover that this is the door into the kingdom of Heaven," says St. John Chrysostom. He does not go on to say that God sometimes locks this door. I don't see any good reason to think that He would. As far as I can tell, in my limited experience, it is always there for us to open. And the Being we discover when we open it is not some energy or "force." What we meet and try to identify with at the heart's deepest point is a sublime awareness—what, in our faith, we call God.

I eagerly look forward to hearing from you soon, my dear friend.
Stafford

* * * * * * * * * * *

March 16, 2010
Dear John,

I've just read the first 10 1/2 pages of your article on Newman. What an engaging and empathic mind Newman had! As I've done before, I congratulate you on your remarkably clear presentation of sometimes difficult and profound thought. I especially enjoyed your defense of the Trinity against those strict monotheists who would have God loving only Himself, because that was all there was in existence to love.

I think the early Church missed something in this regard, incidentally. I've attached a piece published in NCR a year or so ago on God the

Mother. At one level you will not like what I say, but at another, unless I've overlooked something, you will have to grant the point. In any case, we are in complete agreement that the divine life would be eternal hell if God existed in perpetual isolation with no one to love at his own level but Himself.

Stafford

*   *   *   *   *   *   *   *   *   *   *   *

March 16, 2010
Dear Stafford,

I read your article on the feminine in God. My question to you in response is this: what is the problem for Christian theism? Every Christian theologian I have ever read says that God is beyond male and female, and that therefore we use metaphorical language in calling Him Him. To say that we can also call Him Her, like John Paul II did, is not to overthrow Christian theism, but to exploit a possibility that has always been implied in the metaphorical use of gender terms about God. But I almost get the impression from your article that you think that male and female can be said not just metaphorically but literally of God. In this case it is much more problematic to call God Him, and much closer to real error. But surely you don't want to say that God is male and female in the same literal sense in which He exists, creates, or is personal. Male and female are surely only mixed perfections, like courage, and therefore predicable only metaphorically of God, I would think. When it comes to the God-man, of course, maleness is not longer a metaphorical but an entirely literal predication. I realize that you depart from Christian theism, but I don't think that this gender issue is the main point for you.

I would just add that insofar as you mean to affirm the necessarily interpersonal life of God and the absurdity of a solitary God, I entirely agree with you. I also agree that the fruitful use of feminine language with reference to God is under-developed in Christian thought.

John

* * * * * * * * * * *

March 16, 2010
Dear Stafford,

I see a misunderstanding setting in. Let me try to identify it so as to set it aside. What I call the divine initiative (in contrast to God responding always only to our initiative) really has nothing to do with God setting some limit on His availability to us and then arbitrarily lifting the limit. With you I hold that the divine goodness is unbounded, so that we can never be in the position of regretting that God is not more generous than He is. I agree that it makes no sense to stress the personal character of God by way of saying that His love is whimsical and arbitrary. So what do I mean by divine initiative?

God takes the initiative in creating us and preserving us. We did not ask to be created; He loved us first, so that our love for Him is always a requital of His prior love. But there is more to the divine initiative: He did not have to create us, He could have created a world without you and me in it, just as He did in fact create this world without creating certain persons whom He might have created. We are mysteriously elected into existence. God's bounty to us in creating us is not just an emanation of His eternal goodness, but there is an element of *gratuity* in it. His goodness is eternal, but His bounty towards us creatures contains a contingent element. He could have chosen other creatures instead of us, but He inscrutably chose us.

Now this element of election and gratuity is not just found at the beginning, but runs throughout all of our relation with God. If He were to choose the Jewish people as a special priestly people, set apart for accomplishing His work of redemption towards all peoples, this would not be surprising; it would just be more of the same inscrutable election that lies at the root of our existence. And if in my own life I were to marvel at the gratuity of, say, God giving you to me as a special friend, this too would be more of the same inscrutable gratuity that began when God created us. Thus God takes the initiative in choosing us for existence; He takes the initiative in salvation history; He takes the initiative in my own personal history. Even my own prayer life is full of gratuity and election, and as I say this has nothing to do with God restraining His goodness. You see, then, why I balk at a conception of a God who only responds to my initiative.

And you see why—to go back to the beginning of our exchange—the idea of a special revelation in which God first acts towards us seems so natural to me, and why I feel no need to press all of religion into a "bottom up" effort of human beings. And you see, too, why I see something depersonalized in religion without revelation, just as I see something depersonalized in religion without gratuity and without election and without divine initiative.

Does this advance the conversation? I look forward to your response. And I am glad to be once again in lively contact with you, my dear friend of more than half a century!

John

* * * * * * * * * * *

March 21, 2010
Dear John,

Your letter does indeed advance the conversation. It helps me see our differences more clearly. And I like the way it circles back to where we started.

I ask myself the question: Did God elect to bring me into existence over other possible beings? Did He love the idea of me, the potential I represented, so much that He at last ganve me my chance? I say "at last" because untold centuries passed before my chance came.

I see this as a possibility—an attractive one—but not as likely as what I'm inclined to believe. I say "inclined" because I find the subject of human origins extremely mysterious and quite beyond our ability to approach with confidence. But here goes.

Because of the groundbreaking research of Ian Stevenson on reincarnation, it seems very likely to me that you and I have paid quite a few visits to this planet before. It's even possible that we've been evolving for a very long time, possibly up from animal status. If so, it seems less likely that

God had us in mind from the beginning than if He created us a mere sixty-something years ago as the intelligent, thoughtful, morally sensitive beings that we sometimes (actually all too seldom) show ourselves to be. Reincarnation aside, it's hard to believe that all run-of-the-mill human beings were the creations of a loving God who cherry-picked each and every one of them for existence while rejecting others.

I'm inclined to believe that we were not so chosen. No blueprint for a future John Crosby existed in the divine mind, but when he appeared on earth, with the divine spark within him giving him life (but not definition), he became precious. And he became more and more precious as he matured into an unusually gifted and good being. Let me put this into different words. I am saying that God gave you life, as he has given all human beings life, but that your chromosomes gave you your identity. I don't think God ever conceived or designed the chromosomal makeup that made you who you were when you came into the world. Nor do I think He placed you in a Catholic mother's womb because He mysteriously favored you over others. So, to use your language, I think He created you as an emanation of his eternal goodness, but not with an element of gratuity to it. To insist on such gratuity, I believe, is to overvalue yourself, as all top-down thinking tends to do. So, consistent with my bottom-up theology, I see the invitation to lead a godly life not as coming down to us from above through some sort of miracle or special revelation, but as growing from within us by virtue of our sacred pedigree, a pedigree that, if nurtured as God intended, would have a good chance of flowering into a being worthy of sharing his kingdom, and if not worthy at the end of this life, then worthy at the end of some future life.

Furthermore, this worthy being, saintly at last and choosing to grow ever more saintly in God's kingdom, would grow *increasingly* lovely to God. A personal relation to Him that is embryonic at the beginning of his journey would mature into a readiness to conform himself perfectly to God's will. And just as when two human persons delight in a common ideal or goal, God and his saint would too, though at a much more developed level—a level that could continue to develop as the soul comprehended more and more of the divine life. So I am not prepared to grant you that there is "something depersonalized in religion without gratuity and without election and without divine initiative." Please understand that I am not questioning your personal relationship to God as it now stands. I am merely saying that you deserve more of the credit for developing it than you give yourself.

As for his choosing the Jews as his special people in salvation history, I side with my father, who thought the early Hebrews chose themselves, then ratified their choice by interpreting it as coming from God. My father was no theologian, but in this instance I think he was correct.

As always, my dear friend, I look forward to your response.
Stafford

* * * * * * * * * * * *

March 27, 2010
Dear Stafford,

I am puzzled at the idea of God giving me life in general, but not my particular identity as this person. You seem to say that God creates the basic elements and forces of nature, but that individuals, including persons, arise on their own, outside of the creative power of God, as if God were as surprised at the persons who emerge as we are. As a result, you seem not to acknowledge a creator-God in anything like the Christian sense. In fact, your god seems to do far less by way of fashioning the world than Plato's Demiurge does. From a Christian point of view your god isn't really God, nor are you and I really creatures, beings who radically exist through God. I say this not to try to refute your position but simply to clarify your relation to Christianity, which was the point of departure for the entire discussion.

I would just add—and still aiming only at clarification—that the Christian view of God and created persons is a vastly more personalist view than your view. The Christian God freely calls each person by name into existence, including the plain and ordinary ones that you think are too insignificant to be individually chosen by God. The Christian God is a "living and seeing" God just through those aspects of gratuity and election that you put into question. In his last years Norrie Clarke gave a lecture here at Franciscan University in which he defended on philosophical grounds the immediate creation of each individual person by God; he was speaking as a Christian philosopher. Newman seems to me to speak out of the heart of Christian revelation in an Anglican sermon on the personal providence of God, which you can find here: www.newman-reader.org/works/parochial/volume3/sermon9.html. The sermon includes this:

> Men talk in a general way of the goodness of God, His benevolence, compassion, and long-suffering; but they think of it as of a flood pouring itself out all through the world, as the light of the sun, not as the continually repeated action of an intelligent and living Mind, contemplating whom it visits and intending what it effects. Accordingly, when they come into trouble, they can but say, "It is all for the best—God is good," and the like; and this does but fall as cold comfort upon them, and does not lessen their sorrow, because they have not accustomed their minds to feel that He is a merciful God, regarding them individually, and not a mere universal Providence acting by general laws. And then, perhaps, all of a sudden the true notion breaks on them, as it did upon Hagar. Some especial Providence, amid their infliction, runs right into their heart, and brings it close home to them, in a way they never experienced before, that God sees them.

I can't give up the hope that you and I will one day share the faith in the living and seeing God of Christian revelation.

I wish you and Monica a blessed Holy Week.

Your devoted friend,
John

* * * * * * * * * * *

April 4, 2010
Dear John,

You are correct in saying that my understanding of God's relation to man is not that of an orthodox Christian—or of an orthodox Jew for that matter. Psalm 139:18 reads, "You had scrutinized my every action, all were recorded in your book, my days listed and determined, even before the first of them occurred " (The Jerusalem Bible). If this is true, then everything I do was seen beforehand. While this view of God's interest in us is at first attractive and certainly personal, it is personal in a sense quite unlike our own experience of personhood. We follow the lives of those we most love because we care intensely about what decisions they make and how they turn out. If we knew in advance everything they would think or do and everything that would ever happen to them, would we love them so well? I don't think so. So I question whether the standard Christian view of God is the best we can imagine.

If, on the other hand, God is "as surprised at the persons who emerge as we are," as you put it, then a more mutually beneficial relationship can emerge. The opening verses of the same Psalm say, "Yahweh, you examine me and know me, you know if I am standing or sitting, you read my thoughts from far away, whether I walk or lie down, you are watching, you know every detail of my conduct" (vv. 1-2). In these verses God is as interested in us as we are in each other. This is so, I imagine, because He did not give us our particular identity or even have us in mind before we emerged. Nor does He know in advance what we will do with our free wills. I imagine God being fascinated by us and delighting in us when we choose to obey his commands, and sorrowing when we don't—in much the same way as we respond to our own children. Anything less than that depersonalizes God and by removing the element of surprise diminishes the divine life.

In this age of science, in which we know that 20% of fetuses spontaneously abort, and a sizable number of those that come to term are deformed or handicapped in ways that strike us as profoundly tragic, it is hard to believe that God had a hand in their creation. It seems much more plausible that He works through the clumsy and thoroughly imperfect mechanism of random biochemical genetic processes. Or do you suppose that God guides the precise sperm out of 300,000,000 to the egg for fertilization? This is possible, of course. Reincarnationists believe that the law of karma selects the most appropriate sperm, and that too is possible.

I would like to see the Catholic Church reexamine the relation between

God and soul. I suspect that God injects spirit into every human fetus at some point in the gestation process, and out of that we emerge and develop, becoming ever more interesting to Him as we mature and ever more gratifying to Him as we obey his commands. What gestates in that material environment—we call it the soul—is worth saving. We are that soul, and we are precious and valued by Him. And we are given as many chances as needed to come to Him and be gathered up into eternal life, if that is what we finally choose. What we do in that life is of course mysterious, but I would be surprised if there were any limit to the degree that we can deepen the divine life we share with Him. We retain our freedom always, and will never be forced to cultivate an intimacy with Him beyond what we desire or are capable of.

Centuries ago the Church declared there was no salvation outside Catholicism. It later revised that stance. It anathematized heliocentrism but later relented. The traditional view of God's relation to us can also be revised, and should be. We might feel a little less important, but that is probably desirable. The critical thing is that we be loved and valued once we come into existence, and the view I recommend makes plenty of room for that.

Let me finally add, John, that all I have said is highly speculative. But no more so, I think, than the church's official view. And my view has the further advantage of advancing a personalism more like the one we have direct experience of. It is therefore more plausible. Sent to my dear friend with a warm Easter blessing,

Stafford

*   *   *   *   *   *   *   *   *   *   *

May 13, 2010
Dear Stafford,

I've finally filed my grade report, so now I can turn back to the issues that most concern me. At the end of this month I'll be participating at a conference in Rome organized by my son's Dietrich von Hildebrand Legacy Project. You can read about it at www.hildebrandlegacy.org. The conference centers around von Hildebrand's *The Nature of Love,* just out in my translation of it.

The sexual scandals in the Church, and most of all the pattern of coverup by bishops, inflict a terrible wound on the Church. I don't think I've yet fully taken in the gravity of this scandal. I don't at all agree with those who think that a malicious press is persecuting the church; whatever the subjective intentions of particular journalists, the aggressive reporting is bringing to light patterns of sin in the church that would otherwise never come to light, and to that extent the aggressive reporting is functioning as the instrument of a much-needed purification of the church. I was glad to see Pope Benedict acknowledging this on Tuesday when he said that the suffering of the church is more inflicted on the church by the sins of her members than by enemies on the outside. As John Allen pointed out in NCR, the pope thereby distanced himself in an unusual way from all his cardinals and bishops who have been portraying him as the victim of anti-Catholic hostility.

By the way, you'll be interested in Allen's report on the pope's address in Lisbon yesterday on "the Church in the modern world." One sees from this address how strongly Benedict respects certain "acquisitions" of modernity and takes them into his understanding of Christianity. I completely agree with the pope on this and I now dissociate myself from his traditionalist critics.

To pick up the thread of our conversation on what is and what is not Christian. It is true that something would be lost in our relations to other persons if we knew how everything in their lives would turn out. This is, I think, because we would no longer be participants with them in their lives but would stand somehow outside of them as spectators. Our knowledge of their future would be bought at the price of distance and detachment from their lives. But I don't see that this distance and detachment necessarily goes with divine omniscience, and for this reason. If we assume that God does not exist in time but dwells in an eternal present, then His omniscience must mean something entirely different from what omniscience in a time-bound human being would mean. Omniscience in Him may not have the effect of interfering with His dwelling in our midst. Just as theologians speak of the interpenetration of God's immanence in the world and His transcendence over it, so there may be a way in which the divine omniscience interpenetrates the presence of God in our midst–a way in which the divine omniscience does not establish God with "a view from nowhere," but lets Him live in closest solidarity with us, as a full participant in our lives.

Certainly at the level of religious imagination and religious experience, believers have no difficulty invoking God as "Emmanuel" and at the same time as "Father almighty." In fact, to my religious sensibility the omniscience and omnipotence of God has always seemed to make possible a totality of self-entrustment, an unconditional self-entrustment that would not make sense in relation to a god limited in knowledge and power. Thus on me these divine attributes have an effect just the opposite of setting God at a distance from me. So if at the level of religious experience God's omniscience coheres with His being in our midst, being with us and for us in all the circumstances of our lives, then perhaps the two divine attributes can be seen to cohere just as well at the level of theological reflection.

I see here a problematic aspect of your "bottom up" approach to religion. This approach means, you have explained, that God does not take the initiative and come to man, revealing Himself to him, but lets Himself be sought by human beings who find Him out and join themselves to Him by means of their own efforts. But the "bottom up" approach also has, as I now see, another aspect, namely an anthropomorphic tendency. You take knowledge of the future, observe that too much of it in a human being does not befit the human condition, and then you infer that God too must lack knowledge of the future. You moved in a similar bottom up way a while back in our exchange: you observed that human beings can't focus on many different things at the same time, and thence you inferred that God too cannot give His undivided attention to different places in the universe at the same time. This explains why I keep getting the sense of an oppressive finitude about your god. It seems to be a god that is in many ways just an enlarged human being. Even as enlarged he/she seems to me to remain all-too-human.

I recently gave a paper at a conference on the thought of Edith Stein; my paper was in defense of her idea that each person has not only a human essence, but also an individual essence as being *this unrepeatable person*. This individual essence, she argues, is not acquired along the way, it is not something that accumulates throughout the history of an individual person, but it is given from the beginning, just like human nature is not acquired along the way but given from the beginning. I can live up to my individual essence, and live it to the full, or I can fall away from it and fail to achieve it, just as I can fulfil or betray my human nature. (My individual essence, as Edith Stein understands it, is of course something more fundamental than my genetic makeup.) Now if this conception, which I have defended on philosophical grounds, is true, then what would prevent us from adding a theological dimension like this: it is God who creates me as this person; my individual essence is imparted to me by Him at my creation; it is an aspect of the image of God in me. Indeed, it is hard to see how else my individual essence should arise. For it is not a developmental product, but is rather an a priori factor in relation to any and all development; it precedes and conditions all development.

This is a conception that stands in contrast with your view, for you say that God injects some not yet personal "spirit" into the fetus and waits to be surprised by the person that emerges. Again you seem to me to be thinking of God too much according to human patterns. For what you describe fits human procreation well enough; the parents express their love and wait to be surprised by the child who appears. But it stands to reason that God's creative activity will be more radical and encompassing than our human procreative activity. It seems to me that God is more truly God by calling a person by name into being.

It also seems to me that the relation between God and a person thus called by Him into being is an eminently personal relation. For on your view, there is still a certain factor of the "luck of the draw," there is something that occurs outside of God, which is why He is surprised by the result. There is still an element of luck and chance at the origin of each human person. But on my view a person is more radically known and chosen as this person. The divine love does not kick in only after the person has come into existence, but it is the source of the person coming into existence. Rather than trying to work these thoughts through to greater clarity, I'll send them to you raw, thinking that they will at least serve to keep our conversation going.

Your devoted friend, united with you in the search for the truth about God,
John

*   *   *   *   *   *   *   *   *   *   *

May 15, 2010
Dear John,

It is good to hear from you again. Let me get right to the point.

I think it is a mistake to think of God as existing in an Eternal Now, with nothing new ever happening for Him to know. I know that medieval scholasticism developed this view of God, but I don't find it attractive or plausible. Not that it regulates how I think, but it doesn't strike me as consistent with the Judaeo-Christian God, who seems constantly surprised (and sometimes outraged) at what we do in time—so much so that He even appears to change his mind. The God of the Eternal Now is classically framed in Non-Dualist Vedantic Hinduism, and I've made a professional living trying to unseat that God. Hindus of that school have such a low esteem of time-bound reality that they refer to it as maya, or semi-real. I do not share their perspective, nor do I think you do. But it suggests the underlying reason that you and I differ in our views of God's temporality, as well as his omniscience.

I think of God as existing in time. Time, as I see it, is not some Kantian projection of our minds on numinous reality. It is not one of the categories. This is not to say that the way God lives in time is exactly like the way we do. But it is analogous. As a result, his omniscience isn't what you imagine it to be. Knowing what free beings will do in the distant future is not a possible thing to know, not even for God to know.

Thus there are limits to his knowledge—limits that do not work the mischief in my spiritual life that they would appear to work in yours. I would even go so far as to question Kant's view of space as a category. I find the graded materialism of Zeno and the other early Stoics profoundly attractive. The materiality of God is of course so rarified that we cannot imagine it—indeed it is misleading to call it material, perhaps substantive would be safer. What ever you call it, it seems to me that it has to exist in some version or other of space. "Spiritual substance" understood in the way Christians speak of it seems to me oxymoronic.

You will say that I am being anthropomorphic when I speak in this way. And you are correct up to a point, though I think I've been careful to suggest the ways that God transcends our experience. A better word for getting at what I am saying is theomorphic. In trying to imagine how God might go about creating, and what might motivate the way He creates, I take very seriously the notion of his creating us in his image. He puts us in time because He Himself exists in time. He places us in space because He Himself exists in space. We confront and deal with one problem at a time because He does too, though his problems, and his vision, are of course immense in scope and scale. Can he give his attention to my little dilemmas at the same time as he concerns himself with a planet whose sun is about to be swallowed up by a black hole? Does he have as many heads as there are prayers being addressed to him by quadrillions of his creatures? Do all these heads work simultaneously, all of them processing the prayers coming up from all his planets? I'm inclined to think he has only one head because that's all we have. (I'll say more about petitionary prayer at a later date.) For the same reason I'm inclined to think we are free to do evil because even He is free to do it—though I confidently trust he won't. And so on. I especially want to claim that God is not really a He, but a He/She, our Father as well as our Mother. I don't mean this in a metaphorical sense either. I think that God the Father and God the Mother are locked in an eternal embrace, each a distinct persona, though sharing the same divine nature (homoousios). God has never been lonely, not in all eternal time: the two persons have each other. Nor did He/She create the universe out of nothing (ex nihilo), but out of themselves, analogous to the way we procreate. You might even say that the divine core (the soul) that God injects into matter when He/She creates us, individual by individual, is analogous to the sperm that fertilizes the egg. The reason that human beings are divided into two sexes is that God is too. Again, we are made in his/her image. All this, of course, is highly speculative; but to me plausible and to a degree attractive.

Let me now come to the point you make that attracts me. You say that God knows us and names us and treasures us long before we ever come to be and continues to do so once we exist. That would be nice, but is it critical? Would you have felt more loved by your mother or father if they had known and named and treasured you before you were conceived? I don't see why this should be so. You argue that if we are not, then we are not

{30}

unique and unrepeatable. I take your point very seriously; I share your high evaluation of unique and unrepeatable persons. But I think that from the point that God plants something of Him/Herself in the gross matter of the human egg, and we are conceived, we become unique and unrepeatable—and precious. We, after all, are divine. We are not made of nothing; we are chips or slivers of the divine substance itself. The sliver that is you— your soul—is not me, and never will be. Your journey through space and time will never be like anyone else's. I do not find this oppressive in the least.

You say that in my view "There is still an element of luck and chance at the origin of each human person," and this troubles you. It troubles me too, John, and I devoutly wish it were not so. Does God's placing innocent babes in the wombs of crack mothers strike you as an expression of divine love? Do you believe that God selected just this precise soul, and none other, to be born into a favela in Rio? This looks like "luck and chance" to me. Apparently God has a reason for allowing these appalling events to happen. As you know, I've wrestled with the problem of undeserved evil all my life, and I've solved the problem enough to meet my own spiritual needs. (This is not the place to go into it.) But I have not solved it on the backs of innocent children. I believe that God loves each of them, but not in the way we might imagine. "Luck and chance" have their place in the divine scheme. I trust that all will be well in the end, but God expects us to do everything we can to clean up the mess that luck and chance have laid at our door.

The only potential weakness in my system (as I see it)—in my theology as I've much too quickly presented it here—has to do with my need to be known by Him/Her in prayer. This is the way I work it out. Since my very essence, my soul, is divine, the best prayer is the one that puts me in contact with my deepest and truest self. To "grow my soul" is the very essence of religion; it is the destiny that God desires for all of us. If we get the job done, we will inherit the kingdom and enjoy eternal life with our Mother and Father. My best prayer, my mantra, goes like this: "Divine Heart, be present and active within me always." Bottom up? So it seems to me. Deep prayer is hard work, and the payoff is redemption—not by Jesus' dying on the cross, but by the way we deal with our own and others' suffering. The weakness that I just referred to is my tendency to project God outward, when I should really be sinking down deep within where He/She truly resides. The Catholic movement that champions centering prayer addresses this tendency in Christians head-on. I'm working at it.

All the best to my dear friend,
Stafford

P.S. Attached is a more carefully worked out presentation of the Father-Mother God briefly referred to above.

*　*　*　*　*　*　*　*　*　*　*

May 23, 2010
Dear Stafford,

I entered into this exchange with the intention of understanding better your theological position and how it stands in relation to Christianity. Our exchange has achieved this goal. I think I understand better than ever your religious position. It diverges more than I had thought from the Christian faith.

Let me make some remarks on your last message; perhaps we can go still further in understanding each other. If I thought that the divine eternity implies that the temporal world is something unreal, a kind of veil or *maya*, I would also balk at it, but I don't think that it has any such implication. Do you know Norris Clarke's idea of the "dyadic structure" of the human person? He wants to say that the more a person is gathered into himself, recollected, centered, then the wider and deeper the reach of his relations with other persons and other beings. The more I dwell within myself, the greater my "ecstatic" capacity of being present to others. If we try to understand God through the prism of this dyadic structure in human persons, then the divine eternity seems to cohere with all that we want to say about God's presence and activity in our midst. For the divine eternity seems to express a divine measure of recollection, of being gathered into one; God dwells with Himself in such a way that He never yields up His life to the past, or awaits it from the future. We live in the disintegration of temporality because of the creaturely measure of our self-presence. God does not, however, become distant to us as a result of His divine self-presence, any more than animals become distant to us as a result of the fact that we dwell with ourselves in a way in which they cannot dwell with themselves. We can resist the disintegration of time in ways in which the animals cannot; but that just empowers us to be more present to the animals, not less. And so if God, being God, is completely withdrawn from the disintegration of time, He may well, in accordance with the dyadic structure of being, be thereby–precisely thereby—empowered to be present to us with unimaginable closeness.

In one point you take me by surprise: you seem to have abandoned the matter-spirit dualism that I had always taken to be a point of agreement between us. You used to defend the immateriality of the spiritual soul in human beings, but now that you have God being material and occupying space, I can only suppose that you think the same way about the human soul. In fact, you say that a spiritual substance is an oxymoron. For my part, the old arguments still convince me. The exteriority of matter spread out in space is antithetical to the interiority of centered self-presence. I'd like to understand better what it was that turned a resolute dualist into a materialist. (The talk of "rarified matter seems to me nothing but the nostalgia of a former dualist for the concept of immaterial spirit.)

I was struck by your expression that we exist as chips and slivers of the divine substance itself. This is the clearest statement I have heard from you rejecting what Christians call the creaturehood of human persons. We Christians don't think we are ontologically divine. We participate in divine life without literally being divine. Last time I wrote that you seem to me to conceive of God as an enlarged human being and so to obscure the transcendence of God over human beings: this time I am saying that you seem to obscure the divine transcendence in another way, namely by elevating man to divine status and eliminating our creaturehood. The two trains of thought converge so as to abolish the Christian duality of God and creature, or so it seems to me when I read and reread you.

Sometimes your sense of your divinity seems to me to express itself in a way that almost puts into question the otherness of God and to smack of a kind of monistic identification of yourself and God, as when you write: "Since my very essence, my soul, is divine, the best prayer is the one that puts me in contact with my deepest and truest self. To grow my soul is the very essence of religion." The I-Thou encounter with God seems to give way here to an I-me encounter. I agree with you that we find God deep within and not primarily out there in the cosmos, but Christians insist that it is God and not just myself, not even my deepest and truest self, that I encounter within. My deepest self resonates indeed with every glimpse and scent of God, but Christians want to say that the encounter with God in prayer is fundamentally and inalienably dialogical, and cannot be resolved into some deep self-experience. Just as, on your account, the divine father and the divine mother are inalienably two and not one, so it is, as it seems to me, with God and each human being. Perhaps in the end we would not disagree on this point, or what do you say? More than once I have been puzzled at your idea of self-redemption, which reappears here in your last paragraph. We grow our soul, you say, by the way we choose to deal with our own sufferings and those of others. We need no redeemer, but we redeem ourselves. Perhaps you know the memorable passage in the *Apologia* where Newman speaks of the fallenness of the world and its need of a redeemer. Let me quote it here, so we can refer to it in our subsequent exchanges:

> Starting then with the being of a God, (which, as I have said, is as certain to me as the certainty of my own existence, though when I try to put the grounds of that certainty into logical shape I find a difficulty in doing so in mood and figure to my satisfaction,) I look out of myself into the world of men, and there I see a sight which fills me with unspeakable distress. The world seems simply to give the lie to that great truth, of which my whole being is so full; and the effect upon me is, in consequence, as a matter of necessity, as confusing as if it denied that I am in existence myself. If I looked into a mirror, and did not see my face, I should have the sort of feeling which actually comes upon me, when I look into this living busy world, and see no reflexion of its Creator. This is, to me, one of those great difficulties of this absolute primary truth, to which I referred just now. Were it not for this voice, speaking so clearly in my conscience and my heart, I should be an atheist, or a pantheist, or a polytheist when I looked into the world. I am speaking for myself only;

and I am far from denying the real force of the arguments in proof of a God, drawn from the general facts of human society and the course of history, but these do not warm me or enlighten me; they do not take away the winter of my desolation, or make the buds unfold and the leaves grow within me, and my moral being rejoice. The sight of the world is nothing else than the prophet's scroll, full of lamentations, and mourning, and woe.

To consider the world in its length and breadth, its various history, the many races of man, their starts, their fortunes, their mutual alienation, their conflicts; and then their ways, habits, governments, forms of worship; their enterprises, their aimless courses, their random achievements and acquirements, the impotent conclusion of long-standing facts, the tokens so faint and broken of a superintending design, the blind evolution of what turn out to be great powers or truths, the progress of things, as if from unreasoning elements, not towards final causes, the greatness and littleness of man, his far-reaching aims, his short duration, the curtain hung over his futurity, the disappointments of life, the defeat of good, the success of evil, physical pain, mental anguish, the prevalence and intensity of sin, the pervading idolatries, the corruptions, the dreary hopeless of irreligion, that condition of the whole race, so fearfully yet exactly described in the Apostle's words, "having no hope and without God in the world," all this is a vision to dizzy and appal; and inflicts upon the mind the sense of a profound mystery, which is absolutely beyond human solution.

What shall be said to this heart-piercing, reason-bewildering fact? I can only answer, that either there is no Creator, or this living society of men is in a true sense discarded from His presence. Did I see a boy of good make and mind, with the tokens on him of a refined nature, cast upon the world without provision, unable to say whence he came, his birthplace or his family connexions, I should conclude that there was some mystery connected with his history, and that he was one, of whom, from one cause or other, his parents were ashamed. Thus only should I be able to account for the contrast between the promise and the condition of his being. And so I argue about the world; if there be a God, since there is a God, the human race is implicated in some terrible aboriginal calamity. It is out of joint with the purposes of its Creator. This is a fact, a fact as true as the fact of its existence; and thus the doctrine of what is theologically called original sin becomes to me almost as certain as that the world exists, and as the existence of God.

There seems to me to be a profound realism, and a depth of human feeling, in Newman's idea that the world is not in the condition in which it was created, but has been affected by some terrible aboriginal calamity. It seems to me just more of the same realism when he and others go on to say that the evil in which the world lies cannot be alleviated by schemes of education or even by techniques of meditation, but is rather absolutely beyond human solution. The idea of bottom-up redemption, that is, the idea that plans devised only by human beings and supported only by their resources, can suffice to repair the rupture between the world and God seems to me utterly unreal, to speak again with Newman. To my mind it lacks depth and seriousness.

One more thought. You ask whether I would feel more loved by my parents if they had known me and named me before I was conceived. Perhaps not, because I don't expect my parents' love for me to have all of the characteristics of God's love for me. You quoted in an earlier letter this from Psalm 139: "Yahweh, you examine me and know me, you know if I am standing or sitting, you read my thoughts from far away, whether I walk or lie down, you are watching." I don't want to be exposed like this to the sight of my parents or of any other human being; it would be oppressive for me, and would in no way enhance their love for me. I am not disappointed if my parents are not present to me as only God can be present to me, but I am disappointed if God is not present to me as only God can be present to me.

As for the reign of accident that seems to surround the conception of human beings, I acknowledge this as a great difficulty for a personalist thinker. But let us see where the difficulty lies. On my view and the view of most Christians God directly creates each person at conception, even in the case of rape; the secondary causes at work in conception are unable to bring a new person into being. So the difficulty is not that persons originate entirely by accident and apart from the choice of God, for they do not originate in this way. The difficulty is that there is a large factor of the accidental in the secondary causes at work in conception. If these are in some sense co-causes of a new human being, then there is a factor of accident at the origin of many human beings. The difficulty is to understand the cooperation of divine choice and the rolling of the genetic dice. Does this seem to you the correct way of posing the problem?

A blessing on your Sunday, and best wishes to Monica. I'll assume that no news about Louis means that he is holding his own. Greet him from me.

Your devoted friend,
John

* * * * * * * * * * *

June 1, 2010
Dear John,

It is good to get back in harness as we search for a way to bridge our differences. Your latest message was the richest, most challenging, and most helpful. You have pressed me against the ropes. But you have also, in loving brotherly fashion, tried to throw me a lifeline. Let's see what comes of it.

First I'll respond to your view of God's eternity. You say that "the divine eternity seems to express a divine measure of recollection, of being gathered into one; God dwells with Himself in such a way that He never yields up His life to the past, or awaits it from the future." In other words, God doesn't experience time as we do. I would agree up to a point. But if you mean by this that God does not experience duration, I would have to disagree. I have no idea what durationlessness would even mean. There is nothing analogous in human experience to it. But your notion of God's experiencing all events, past and present, in an eternal now, well, that is at least barely comprehensible. But where is the evidence for it? And why do you think such a mode of awareness superior to one ensconced in time? God is divine enough for my needs if He can evoke the past at will with no weakening in intensity. As for the future, well, as I see it, not even God can know something that hasn't happened yet. That would be like being able to create a square circle, a logical impossibility except in the halls of science fiction. Even if it were possible, I would see this kind of omniscience as a curse, for it would deprive God the delight of experiencing newness. I don't question your defense, incidentally, of God's presence to us "with unimaginable closeness." More on that now.

You were right to suspect that we might not be far apart when it comes to my claim that there is an inner divinity coiled in the depths of our being. I don't mean that we are in any full sense the very God of the universe. That would be to go too far—much too far. But to be content to speak of our relationship with God as Buber speaks of it—I to Thou—is not to go far enough. For however close you and I are to each other, or as I am to Monica or to any of my children, God is closer. Billy Graham puts it nicely when he writes that God "planted something of himself within us" when He created us. God is not within us merely as a permanent cherished guest who is always available to us when we need Him, an I to a Thou. We are, it seems to me, his seedlings. The seedling is not the parent tree, but it shares the same nature. It is this metaphysical intimacy that makes prayer possible. God and ourselves are much more closely related than we are to our pets. Our pets have no idea what it is like to be us, but we have a very, very limited awareness of what it is like to be God; for, like us, God is a person. And the more grounded we are in meditation and prayer, the deeper we go, the more of God's inner experience opens up to us, until, in the case of a mystic like Meister Eckhart, it is as if the boundaries separating Him from us dissolve for a moment. Eckhart writes, "The eye with which I see God is the same eye with which God sees me. My eye and God's eye are one eye, one seeing, one knowing, and one loving." Of course the boundaries do not really dissolve, for we are forever locked in a relation of creaturely dependence. Nevertheless, God, in an act of *noblesse oblige*, deigns to share a small part of Himself with us if we want it. I am very curious to know if you would accept this important qualification and clarification—a clarification I owe to your incisive critique, incidentally.

Now we come to the question of bottom-up redemption, back to where we started months ago. Thank you for the quote from Newman. His words are stirring and perhaps unparalleled in their depiction of human wretchedness. But they overlook the many examples of human sanctity, and the many more of ordinary human decency. I think Newman is wrong when he speaks of God's being ashamed of his children on earth, like the young man "cast upon the world without provision." God has hidden Himself from us so we can develop our creaturely independence and come to Him freely when we are ready—whether in this world or some future one. If God provided us with all we needed to develop without much struggle into saints, what value would there be in our accomplishment? As I see it, God gave us the natural ability, by virtue of his seed-like presence in our souls, to choose Him—if we want. There are plenty of hints of his presence in our world, starting with the sheer beauty of natural landscapes, to get us started. And there are the teachings left us by an army of saints and sages in almost every culture. We are not altogether unprovisioned. In fact most of the world's educational systems encourage good citizenship and ethical dealing. Newman is developing one side of the human condition in these quotations. It seems to me that the Church has too much emphasized this side—to the extent of claiming that our only hope comes via supernatural intervention from Heaven, that is, Jesus's death on the cross.

Finally, we come to my presumed rejection of spirit-matter dualism. Let me clarify. All I've done is given the mind-body problem a little toehold toward solution. The weakness of standard substance dualism, as you know, is that the interaction between the immaterial soul and the material body is inexplicable. But what if the soul were material in some exquisitely subtle sense that allowed it to interact with its clumsy shell (the body) while not sharing its inevitable fate (death)? This is the metaphysics of ancient Stoicism, and I find it attractive. Even God, for these Stoics, was material in some exalted sense—because nothing existed that was not in some sense material. As I see it, God in Heaven can be seen, which means that He has a body that is in some gloriously refined sense material. I hope you see now how I use the word. The gross materiality of the physical world is not the stuff out of which the soul is made. They are as removed from each other as a lump of coal from an apparition of the Virgin. I am still very much a dualist, though without the sharp edges.

Let me close by telling you that your critique helped me work through a problem I was having with prayer. An analogy might help. My soul is like a lamp lit by electricity. God is like the power plant supplying the electricity which lights me up when I turn on the switch. I was in danger of confusing God with the electricity and overlooking its source. I now see a real difference between classical meditation and prayer. In meditation we experience the electricity that lights us up—a good thing. In prayer we "travel up the line" to the source of the electricity—a better thing.

Every blessing to you, my dear friend. I look forward to your next missive. Stafford

*   *   *   *   *   *   *   *   *   *   *   *

July 1, 2010
Dear Stafford,

I don't like making you wait too long for a response, because I know that this can knock some of the momentum out of our exchange. On the other hand, I want very much to avoid the old polemical tit-for-tat, and the best way I can do that is to take my time, trying to hear all that you are saying, trying to learn from it.

I read your article with great interest on the different views of Moksha found in the three great schools Vedanta, and I found myself in agreement with all of the criticisms you make of the three views. Regarding the divine eternity, I assume with you that there is duration in the divine consciousness. As I understand it—who really understands it?—temporal duration is one mode of duration, but not the only one. You ask why non-temporal duration would be superior to temporal duration. I would think that temporal duration involves a certain disintegrated existence that befits creatures but not God. Aquinas says somewhere that time-bound beings exist with something of themselves outside of themselves, and he explains by saying that some of their being is no more, and some is not yet. That implies a deficit of self-possession, and seems un-divine. In ch. 8 of *The Selfhood of the Human Person* I examine different types of deficient self-possession, and I consider how it is that they imply creaturely, non-divine personhood.

In ch. 3 of that book I consider what the spiritual masters have called recollection, and I argue that the deeper our recollection goes, the more we rise above the disintegration of temporality. If we draw out this ascending line, we can almost glimpse how a supremely powerful self-presence and self-possession would no longer yield anything to a past, or await anything from a future. This is what lies behind the Christian idea that for God to be God, He/She must not be in time like we are in time. When you say that it is intrinsically impossible to know the future, and thus even impossible for God, you say what would be true if God were time-situated like you and I are, but what may not be true if the divine duration excludes temporal existence. As for God being deprived of the experience of newness, I would think that there is always newness in the freedom of persons, and that God therefore experiences newness in us. But He experiences it without the index of surprise, which is the aspect under which we time-bound creatures typically experience it.

I grant you that God is much more incomprehensible if Christians are right about his eternal duration, than if you are right about His temporality. Every time I have objected to you that you have too anthropomorphic a view of God, I have in effect been saying that He/She is more incomprehensible than you allow. But there is a Christian significance to this incomprehensibility: just because God is so utterly other than we human beings, we need some icon or image of God if we are to know Him; we need the God-man. The mystery of the divine otherness blocks once and for all a bottom up approach to God; we cannot with our own wit and genius and resourcefulness find Him out. He has to turn to us, uttering a word that we can understand. Without some mediator sent by Him, He remains in His unapproachable light. This is why revelation is such a fundamental category of Christian existence. If I understand you rightly, revelation plays no role at all in your conception of religion.

As this conversation between us goes on, I see more and more clearly this connection: what I call the recurring anthropomorphic tendency of your religious thinking, makes revelation superfluous, whereas my recurring protest against anthropomorphism goes hand in hand with religion based on revelation.

I have not yet responded to other important issues that you raise, but since I have to leave tomorrow morning for several days, I'll send you now what I have as a down payment for more when I return, rather than make you wait still longer.

God bless you, Stafford. Tomorrow Pia and I celebrate our 33rd wedding anniversary! She sends her love.

John

* * * * * * * * * * *

July 7, 2010
Dear Stafford,

Many thanks for your anniversary greetings. Pia and I often recall with amusement the redwood tree you gave us as a wedding present that was meant to live for hundreds of years, and made it only a few weeks.

Will you by chance be in Mobile in early August? Pia is donating a kidney to my sister Lynn, who is in renal failure. The surgery will be in New Orleans on August 3. We have to stay around for a final medical exam on August 12. Pia may be well enough to move around by August 8 or 9, and if she is we will come to Mobile for a visit of a few days. It would be wonderful if this visit would coincide with one of your visits home.

Let me just add to my last message that I agree with you that the I-Thou encounter, important as it is in all deeper prayer, does not fully capture the relation between God and man. The fact that we exist through God, and hence exist as a kind of offspring of God, adds something that is not contained in the I-Thou relation, which can after all exist between two persons who in no way owe their existence to each other. Buber would perhaps retort that each person in that relation does in a sense owe his existence to the other, for Buber often stresses that it is not the case that my I is first constituted and enters only later into relation with a Thou, but that it is constituted in and through that relation. But I would hold, and I think you would too, that what Buber really means, or what he should limit himself to saying, is that we enable each other to be actualized as persons by encountering each other as personal subject. But God does more for us than actualize us as persons; He calls us into being as persons. He creates the possibility of our actualization by first giving us our very being. As a result we have a mysterious "consanguinity" with God. (I write about this in ch. 9 of *The Selfhood of the Human Person*.) You are right that there is an intimacy with God in prayer that is rooted in this consanguinity. So this is an important point of agreement between us.

I would also grant you that this consanguinity should keep us from going too far in affirming the otherness of God. If we are "of His stock," then we must bear some resemblance to Him. So when Christians argue for the necessity of revelation, as I did in the first part of this letter, we should take care not to imply that we would have to be agnostics if we did not have revelation.

I wonder, however, if your view of this consanguinity is not bound to be in some sense weaker than the Christian view, given your idea that persons arise by natural causes working apart from the direct creative activity of God, even to the point that they "surprise" God when He first comes to know them. The Christian view of the direct creation of each person by God seems to imply that God puts more of Himself in to each person whom He creates, more of Himself than He does on your view of the more naturalistic way in which persons emerge into being.

I can't make friends with the idea of God and the soul consisting of "rarefied matter." You seem to me here to be reversing the path of Augustine, who struggled for years to free himself from a materialistic view of the soul and of God. (The matter invoked by the Manicheans was also "rarefied." Recall the divine sparks and fragments contained in plants and foods, as related by Augustine in the *Confessions*.) The talk of "rarefied matter" seems to me curious; it seems to mean "highly spiritualized matter," or "matter which is hardly matter any more." It seems to be the language of a materialist who knows better and has a bad conscience about his materialism! In any case, your main motive seems to me questionable, namely the motive of taking the edge off the mind-body mystery. For you take away one mystery by introducing a brand new one, namely the mystery of how subjectivity and freedom can after all be perceptible to the bodily senses, or at least in principle perceptible to them through some enhancement of them. I think that your way of coping with the mind-body mystery is fraught with at least as many difficulties as the idealist way of coping with it (saying that matter exists only in its being-perceived by a mind). In fact, in some ways the idealist position makes more sense to me. I for my part am willing simply to live with the mystery of matter-spirit union in us human beings. Do you know the work of Colin McGinn, a non-Christian philosopher who calls his view of the mind-body union a "mysterian" position, on the grounds that we human beings will never be able to understand how mind and body can touch and interpenetrate?

I see I have addressed mainly your view of the human soul as material, but not of God as material. Maybe we can come back to that. When we do, you can be sure that I will raise the anthropomorphism issue again.

I am glad that you found useful the distinction between what God works in us, and God Himself who works it.

I'm sure I have said more than enough to provoke many responses from you, and I look forward to receiving them.

Let us entrust our exchange to the mercy of God, imploring Him to enlighten us as we go.

Blessings to you and Monica,
John

*   *   *   *   *   *   *   *   *   *   *   *

July 13, 2010
Dear John,

It is tempting to tie in a visit home with your presence there. Monica and I will be doing a walking tour of the English Lake District from July 22-29, so I don't know if we will be inclined to travel again so soon. But we will see. Please give my warmest greetings to Lynn. And what a gift from Pia to her sister-in-law!

First let me say that it is always good to discover where we agree, in this case on God's "consanguinity" with us.

I am now going to address your criticism of "transcendental materialism"—a good enough name for my theory of reality. What I will say in the next few paragraphs is taken from a paper published in *International Philosophical Quarterly* in 2004. I've changed very little.

The early Stoics—in particular Zeno of Citium, Cleanthes of Assos, and Chrysippus of Soli, all of them active in the third century B.C.—prefigure my theory in several remarkable ways. First, they were explicitly committed to a thoroughgoing materialism. But Stoic materialism is not the materialism current in philosophical circles today. Contemporary materialists, whether reductive (like Dennett) or non-reductive (like McGinn), feel compelled to reject out of hand belief in God, soul, and what we label today "spiritual beings." In contrast, the early Stoics unanimously confessed belief in an eternal supreme being who rationally governed the universe. They also believed in a multiplicity of lesser gods invisible to us. And they not only believed in souls, but that souls could survive bodily death—Cleanthes holding that all human souls survive, Chrysippus the souls of the wise only.

Stoic materialism might seem absurd on the surface. But deeper study will nullify that too-quick reaction. In the ancient world, theirs was a popular philosophy among thoughtful people, often amounting to a religion, and for good reason. There was no collection of gods who disgraced themselves with their bad behavior. God, for Zeno, was "the *logos* in the matter," "aether, endowed with Mind, by which the universe is governed." "He interpenetrated the whole matter of the world as a *pneuma*." He was the active, organizing principle residing in the passive, originally unorganized matter of the world. Though corporeal himself, the Stoic God was "the aether at its clearest and purest . . . the most mobile thing that exists."

The important thing about Cleanthes and company, for our purposes, is that they consistently embed all real things in matter, right up to deity—an extraordinary innovation for its day. For them there are not two substances, only one. Might they, therefore, be in a better position to take the "scandal" out of Cartesian interaction theory with its sharply opposed, apparently incompatible substances? Carl Jung seems to sympathize with this ancient way of thinking. In 1946 he wrote: "Since psyche and matter are contained in one and the same world, and moreover are in continuous contact with one another and ultimately rest on irrepresentable, transcendental factors, it is not only possible but fairly probable, even, that psyche and matter are two different aspects of one and the same thing." These are not the words of a substance dualist but of a monist, and they perfectly catch the tenor of my theory. Jung is uncomfortable with the black-and-white thinking of conventional dualists, even more so with the reductive theories of contemporary materialists, whom he refers to as "weaker minds" unduly impressed by "the spirit of the age." Jung is staking out a middle ground between these two extremes, and so am I.

I don't see any danger in conceiving God in this manner, John, and it has much to recommend it. As I mentioned in my last letter, God is visible to us in heaven. If that is so, He must be material in some sense. The important thing, as Augustine rightly saw, is to distance the divine matter from the gross forms that envelop us. Actually it is unfortunate that we are stuck with the word "matter." "Substance" is better, so let's use that. I am saying that instead of there being only two kinds of substance, two completely different and incompatible species of substance so to speak, as in conventional dualism, there are many layers, from the densest to the most ethereal, of only one substance. What danger is there in representing God and his creation in this way? There is nothing remotely mortal or concupiscible in the divine substance. Thus Augustine should not be concerned. Further, my theory of a single substance with many layers in it goes well with your view of God's and our consanguinity. We are not only two different expressions of a single genus, the genus we call personhood, but two different expressions of a single genus we call substance. Psychology and metaphysics merge. I know how reluctant we all are to give up a belief we have long held, but doesn't my view of things make good sense, however unorthodox (for our time) it may be?

Now let me introduce a new topic, or rather an old one in a somewhat different context. And let me say at the outset that I would welcome any insight you might have that would help me solve an existential problem. First take a look at the picture attached above.

It's a picture of our galaxy, the Milky Way. It has about 170 billion stars (suns) in it. And it is only one of 100 to 300 billion galaxies in the known universe. (Check out the attached picture of the famous Whirlpool galaxy with its smaller companion.) Here is my concern: Is the God we've been describing here, and that we dare to pray to and feel we have a personal relationship with, the creator and governor of this massive universe? When I meditate on the sheer size of the universe, and the probability that our planet is only one of zillions, I wonder how God could take much interest in me, or even in earth. How far up the line do our prayers go? Do they really reach the pinnacle, the intelligent designer of this stupendous spectacle we name the universe, or do they peter out at lower latitudes? I can understand why the Chinese direct most of their prayers to their ancestors: They would not presume that the Jade Emperor (their name for God on High) would be concerned for their wellbeing. They worship many gods in addition to their ancestors, but these are little more than the equivalent of our saints.

Don't get me wrong. I pray fervently: I thank, I ask for help, and I adore. But I really have very little idea of the nature of the Target. How far do my prayers go? Are they intercepted by beings closer to home?

Now perhaps you see why I am not so quick to assume that God knew me by name before He created me. It seems presumptuous and improbable. I'd feel a lot better if the earth was the center of the universe! Too bad it's not.

Are you ever bedeviled by these concerns? How do you work them out?

Sent with a blessing and a toast to our friendship,
Stafford

* * * * * * * * * * *

July 16, 2010
Dear Stafford,

You raise a very serious existential question: what do we make of the immensity of the cosmos, and especially of the fact that we human beings seem to be, when set within the cosmos, a negligible quantity, a mere speck? Are we too small to be noticed by God? The question is perhaps not as closely tied to contemporary cosmology as one might think, since after all the psalmist says in one place (psalm 8), "When I see the heavens, the work of your hands, the moon and the stars which you arranged, what is man that you should keep him in mind, mortal man that you care for him?" You ask how I make my peace–my personalist peace–with this cosmic immensity.

In ch. 2, section 3, of *The Selfhood of the Human Person*, I explore a related problem, namely the apparent smallness of each human being when considered in relation to the 7 billion human beings presently alive on earth. One seven-billioneth is a very small fraction. I argue that when we come to know a person we find that there is something in him or her that defies the laws of numerical quantity, something that refuses to be relativized by vast numerical quantity. In the encounter with a person I see that he or she is not an infinitesimally small fractional part, but rather exists "as if the only one." I see that a person is never a mere part but a whole of his or her own. I'd be very interested in knowing what you make of these pages in my book. If there is any merit to what I say there, then it seems to follow that there is something in the being of each person that resists cosmic immensity; it seems to follow that the full truth about each person does not lie in his or her cosmic size, and that persons are no more swallowed up by the cosmos than they are swallowed up by vast crowds of people.

This thought has received an immortal expression by Kant in the wonderful passage at the end of the *Critique of Practical Reason*. I quote from memory: there are two things that ever and again awaken the awe of man—the starry sky above him and the moral law within him. He says that standing under the starry sky we feel almost annihilated, so great is our sense of our smallness. But that feeling of smallness is in a way reversed, he says, when we consider our relation to the moral order of the world. Then I become aware, he says, of a certain infinity in myself, and of a destiny beyond earthly-cosmic life. He seems to mean that I exist in two incommensurable realms, in the realm of the physical cosmos, and in the realm of the moral universe. The category of quantity belongs to the former realm, but not to the latter. Thus speck-like smallness only makes sense in the former realm, but it makes no sense in the latter.

If I hold fast to this person-nature duality of my being, and especially to my existing in the moral universe, or existing as a member of the kingdom of ends, as Kant says, then the possibility of an immediacy to God–of "appearing" before Him–begins to make sense. Just as I can pick a person out of 7 billion and consider him or her "as if the only one"–and this not just as an arbitrary act of abstracting from the others but as a way of getting at the truth of the person—so perhaps God can take me, and each other person as well, "as if the only one." It makes a certain personalist sense once the realm of the person is apprehended in all its incommensurability with the physical cosmos.

Now, this way of staying intact as person in light of the immensity of the cosmos, has a great bearing on the other issue you raised, the issue of "transcendental materialism." Perhaps you were thinking of them as separate issues, but in fact something follows for the materialism question from what I have just said. If God is material, then my relation to God is inevitably structured by the category of quantity. For matter, however ethereal and rarefied you try to make it, still takes up space, and is still subject to laws of quantity, such as that the greater part of matter occupies more space and the lesser part less space. The divine immensity becomes a spatial immensity. From this it follows that speck-like being is inescapable for us. Our speck-like smallness has the last word, it gives the full truth about ourselves. There is no other realm where this smallness is replaced by a kind of infinity. Your fear that we humans may be too small to be noticed by God Himself is at this point quite natural. It seems clear to me that your materialism regarding God lends support to this fear, and that the old way of distinguishing matter and spirit helps us to defeat this fear. The incommensurability of realms of which I just spoke is really an incommensurability of matter and spirit. Your materialism would have the effect of annulling this incommensurability.

I'm off next week to the wedding in Washington DC of my son John Henry. He is marrying a really lovely girl whom he has known since his college days. I wish you and Monica well in England. Have you told her about our unforgettable travel in France in the summer of 1965?

In friendship,
John

* * * * * * * * * * *

July 31, 2010
Dear John,

Monica and I are safely back from our trip to England. We walked at least 100 miles in seven days. Often I thought of our trip through France and the wonderful sense of freedom, high spirits, and thrilling conversation we enjoyed together so long ago—was it in 1965? I have spoken often of it to Monica.

There is a lot of ground to cover here. I've been reading your *Selfhood* and now understand you better. I may quote from it later, but first let me remind you of what you wrote a month ago:

"As for God being deprived of the experience of 'newness,' I would think that there is always newness in the freedom of persons, and that God therefore experiences newness in us. But He experiences it without the index of 'surprise,' which is the aspect under which we time-bound creatures typically experience it."

You were arguing that God does not experience events that have happened, or will happen, as happening in the past or future, as we do. If He did, then his self-possession would be limited, and He would be less than God.

Bear with me as I think along a different line. First, look carefully at what you have written. If the phrase "newness in the freedom of persons" has any meaning, is at all intelligible, then God would have to be experiencing us in a present that has just arrived, and that would mean that for Him there was a future—namely the things we would do that we haven't done yet. When I apply the perhaps too human word "surprise" to the divine awareness, I mean this experience of newness. I have no trouble with God's experiencing the universe's unfolding as new, as part of his future, but I have plenty of trouble viewing it in any other way! If God now knows everything that will ever happen in the universe, what a boring life that would be. It would mean, I think, that God is living in eternal hell.

As I see it, the experience of duration is a *divine attribute,* and duration entails the experience of past, present, and future. But God—and here I agree with you—experiences duration in a way quite different from the way we do. We lose track of what happens in time, and we miss it altogether when we sleep. But what distinguishes us from God is not that we are enmeshed in time and He is not, but that we are imperfectly enmeshed in time while He is constantly and universally aware of what is passing. Minerals have no experience of duration, trees perhaps only a little. The higher on the scale of reality one finds oneself, the more perfectly aware of what transpires in time one is. Angels, I hypothesize, do not sleep; they are more perfectly embedded in time than we are. I suspect we will be, too, when we pass on to more ethereal realms following our death. What you object to, I think, is the experience of *tedium* that our time-consciousness involves here on earth. Subtract that, and you begin to approximate the experience of divine duration—an experience with no diminution of memory of past events, and infinite openness and awareness of the unfolding present. Duration of this kind would provide God with a constantly fascinating experience—one that would generate emotions in Him that it would be foolish of us to speculate on.

I also think, incidentally, that space is a divine attribute. Space is where things happen and where God finds Himself, including in us. As you say, "in the deepest recollection I find myself opening to God in the center of my being" (p.170). We exist in space, and so must God if we are to take you at your word. Space is not an alien experience to God, even in his highest heaven.

To sum up my way of thinking about God—as existing in space and time and matter—I can do no better than quote from Pope's great philosophical poem *Essay on Man:* "All are but parts of one stupendous whole,/ Whose body nature is, and God the soul." I take the claim that God made us in his image more literally than you do. You will label my way of thinking anthropomorphic, but I would call it theomorphic: God makes us as much like Himself as He can, and He places us in a world as much like his own as He can. I cannot imagine why God would do otherwise. Bear in mind that many (not me) would call your personalism when applied to God anthropomorphic.

Let us change the subject and come back to the question I raised in my last letter: how we are to think about prayer. In Chapter 2, Section 3, of your book you do a fine job of distinguishing between our numerical smallness and our absoluteness as persons. I agree with you entirely and find a certain consolation in the distinction. It emboldens me to think that the God who created me—the same God who created the universe with its billions of galaxies and probably millions of planets like ours—may know me by name as you and I know each other—as an I confronting and befriending a Thou in a personal encounter. Still, even though I am as committed a personalist as you, I think it more likely that God confronts me and knows me in a manner more mysterious: as the divine seed nestled within me and giving me the chance to form myself as the man I am. It takes some getting used to, but it is this God Within, this immanent God, who hears and responds to my prayers. The deeper I go, the more completely I find Him. Does this way of speaking resonate with you, John? Do you see it as an I-Thou encounter? Or does prayer have meaning for you only if there is an encounter with the transcendent God? I am eager to hear what you have to say on this matter.

Finally, allow me to answer your concern about the philosophy I've labeled "transcendental materialism." You wrote:

"If God is material, then my relation to God is inevitably structured by the category of quantity. For matter, however ethereal and rarefied you try to make it, still takes up space, and is still subject to laws of quantity, such as that the greater part of matter occupies more space and the lesser part less space. The divine immensity becomes a spatial immensity. From this it follows that speck-like being is inescapable for us. Our speck-like smallness has the last word, it gives the full truth about ourselves. There is no other realm where this smallness is replaced by a kind of infinity. Your fear that we humans may be too small to be noticed by God Himself is at this point quite natural. It seems clear to me that your materialism regarding God lends support to this fear, and that the old way of distinguishing matter and spirit helps us to defeat this fear."

For me the divine substance, what Pope calls the soul of the universe, does everything that the soul conceived of as immaterial does. In particular, it doesn't die. Yes, it occupies space. In my view *everything* occupies space. But how does it follow that our speck-like bodies must therefore have the last word? We are no less persons because our souls are material in a manner that distinguishes them from the matter of the body. I would say, with you, that our personhood, our "soulhood," has the last word. The substance out of which it is made is ineffaceable. Someday, let us hope, we will join the transcendent God in the highest heaven, which is made of a substance that we have no knowledge of, and where we will "see God face to face." The important, the critical thing is that the dualism between spirit and nature is left intact. I leave it intact and affirm it with all the passion that you do. I think we are close to making what philosophers call "a distinction without a difference," and that it should not come between us. Let me put it this way: Nothing of any importance about the way I make sense of the world, of God, and of our relation to Him would change if it turned out that the soul, and God, were immaterial after all.

In anticipation of your next letter, I send blessings to you, my dear friend,
Stafford

* * * * * * * * * * * *

August 31, 2010
Dear John,

I came across this in Wordsworth's famous "Ode on the Intimations of Immortality." He addresses himself, "Thou, whose exterior semblance doth belie/Thy soul's immensity."

This is apropos our ongoing discussion and expresses a wonderful insight we agree on completely.

Stafford

* * * * * * * * * * * *

September 1, 2010
Dear Stafford,

I've made you wait far too long, and my only excuse is that since I last heard from you we have had John Henry's wedding and the kidney transplant from Pia to Lynn. And now we have just heard that John and Robin are already expecting. It has been a summer long on family life and short on philosophical work. Thank you very much for the striking line from Wordsworth. How good it is that we share an awe at "the infinite abyss of existence" (Newman) in each person.

I am teaching a course on William James this semester, and I must say that his religious position, and also his genial persona, reminds me very much of you. His finite and time-bound god, his ineradicable religious aspirations, his respect for psychical research all remind me of your own theological position. I appreciate James more than I used to, though I still find that he can lapse into distressingly subjectivist trains of thought (which is not to say that I see the same subjectivism in you). In my course I will explore the kinship of James with Newman, which I think is very considerable.

As for God's relation to time, I find the subject impenetrable. I have no idea how we ought to think of God's relation to his own duration and to our temporality. Just today at mass we had the reading from Proverbs about not inquiring into things too sublime for us, and this is surely one of those things. I will only say that you seem to me, in your last message, to make too quantitative the difference between our duration and God's. For you say that God's time-consciousness is stronger than ours in that it undergoes no breaks, that his memory has no defects, etc. But it would seem to me that His duration-consciousness must be different in kind from ours, and not just stronger by degree. After all, the time-consciousness of a deeply recollected person is stronger not just in degree from the time-consciousness of an unrecollected person (cf. my ch. 3 in *Selfhood*), nor is the time-consciousness of a person stronger just in degree from the time-consciousness of an animal; so I surmise that between God and us the difference is not just one of degree, or a mere quantitative difference, but some difference in kind. As usual in our exchange, where you are content with a difference of degree between God and man, I argue for a difference in kind, or in other words, I see the similarity between God and man as analogical where you see it as literal.

Do you really want to hold that God exists as spatially extended? The arguments for a world of non-extended being—you know them well—seem to me very compelling. Even an author like Colin McGinn is capable of stating them very effectively (as in his *The Mysterious Flame*). In the consciousness of a person, conscious experiences are not spatially related to each other. It makes no sense to speak of my experience of anxiety being above or below, to the left or to the right of my simultaneous experience of deliberating about some matter. It makes no sense to say that one of the experiences takes up more space than the other. And the self that lives in these experiences is not related in any spatial way to them. When I spoke of the deepest center of the recollected person, I was meaning to use a spatial metaphor, not to ascribe literal spatiality to the recollected person. Well, given the non-spatiality of consciousness, I ask you: Why do we have to say that everything is spatially extended, God included, when our own being shows itself in part to be not spatially extended? Why would you conceive of God as more embedded in space than our own consciousness is? You seem to me to take the mode of being most obvious to us bodily humans, namely material being, and to identify that with being as such, and thus to think of God as material and spatially extended. But why should our human bodily senses be commensurate with all of being? Why should there not be being that escapes the reach of the bodily senses? As I say, we do not have to stop with just posing these questions; we can actually find in our own consciousness a realm of being that the bodily senses cannot register. You can imagine how strongly your idea of God's spatial extension reinforces my impression of an all-too-human conception of God in your thought.

You may be right that our difference on this subject is not so great, seeing how you import many of the characteristics of spirit into the matter that you think is spirit. But still, it is a serious question whether matter, characterized by part-outside-of-part, and retaining extensive quantity, can possibly be home to all the characteristics of spirit. For example, in our spirit, when we are recollected, we at the same time dwell within ourselves, and exist ecstatically outside of ourselves in transcending ourselves towards others. Is this interpenetration of within and without possible in a material being? Does it not give evidence of the person living in a way that defies the logic of spatial extension?

As for the immanence of God in my own consciousness, I think that what most corresponds to my experience is a paradoxical interpenetration of divine immanence and divine transcendence. The divine otherness is always present to me, since I believe in a God who acts on His own inscrutable initiative toward me and out of His own inscrutable freedom, as I have written before. Thus I do not experience God, and do not want to experience Him, simply as the principle of growth in my inner life. At the same time, I seek God within, not out in the cosmos, and sometimes I sense within a mysterious familiarity of God that forms the most surprising unity with His transcendence.

John

*　*　*　*　*　*　*　*　*　*　*

September 9, 2010
Dear John,

Congratulations to you and Pia, grandparents-to-be. I trust that the kidney transplant went well for both donor and recipient? My daughter

Southey is also expecting—in December. That grandchild will be my fourth. Any news on Maria?

You are correct to see similarities between James's and my philosophy. What a wonderful course—James and Newman—you are in the midst of!

We are not as far apart in our views of God's time-consciousness as might first appear. The distinction you make between an animal's and our time consciousness is indisputable. But not so much because of a different relation to duration, but because of a different capacity for conscious life in general. Dogs and cats can't reason, can't pray, can't make a moral choice, can't enjoy music or art, and so forth. But they do yawn when bored or sleepy, and they do a lot of waiting for their masters to reappear. Their experience of duration is one of the things we have most in common with them, I should think. To move in the other direction, God's experience of duration is, similarly, one of the things we have most in common with Him. But just as there are enormous differences between a dog's capacity to make a moral act and our own, so is there, and to a far greater degree, between our spiritual and moral capacities and God's.

Yes, I do believe that God exists in space. Space is where things happen in his universe—happen to us, and happen to Him. What is there about space that is deemed fundamentally undivine? You do bring up, however, some challenging points when you enquire about the relation between our conscious experiences and our body. It is certainly true that whatever material element they may have escapes us; an experience of anxiety, as you say, has no physical attributes that we can make out. But it is equally true that *all* our conscious experiences take place in a body. And imagine how great a being we would be if our consciousness extended to all 7 billion human bodies on the planet. The more spatially extended we are, in other words, the more diverse and complete our experience. Now if God is extended in *all* space—and don't we say as much when we call Him omnipresent?—think how unimaginably comprehensive and immense his experience must be. But I do not mean to limit his experience to matter as we know it. God exists, I imagine, in a material heaven that is so ethereal we could not possibly sense it with our gross eyes and ears—in other words, outside the material universe as we know it. In saying this I am admitting what you admit: we have almost no idea what heaven is like. Only in one particular do we part company: heaven, for me, is a realm where beings are distinguished from each other by occupying adjoining spaces; and it is a place whose inhabitants, including God, experience duration. I find nothing unholy in this, and much to recommend it. After all, space and time are where we find ourselves and how we experience ourselves. A first premise in my theology is that God makes us, and our world, as much like his as possible. Why should He not? We are wisely instructed to think of ourselves as made in his image. I would also think He made our world in the image of the place where He dwells—a coarse, blemished facsimile of heaven to be sure, but an image nonetheless. This goes back to our discussion on persons. We are persons because God is a person; He is in the business of making beings as much like Himself as He can. Similarly, we find ourselves in space-time because God exists in space-time. But there is a vast difference *in degree* between his and our personhood; similarly, there is a vast difference in degree between his experience in space-time and ours. His perfection and infinity are protected, but not at the expense of turning Him into Something so strange that we cannot relate to Him—which is what I think Catholic theology tends to do when it insists on a difference *in kind*.

I marvel that two boys who happened to live a few blocks apart in a sleepy southern city where nothing of much importance ever happened are having such a discussion. It wouldn't surprise me if the discussion continued on the Other Side—where things, let us hope, will be much clearer.

Stafford

* * * * * * * * * * * *

October 17, 2010
Dear Stafford,

I just got back from England, where I attended the beatification of Newman on Sunday. You can imagine how much it meant to me to be present at this moment of ecclesial recognition of my father in faith.

I hope I don't impede the flow of the conversation by taking longer to respond than you do. Often I don't see right away the most fruitful way to advance the discussion, and so I let things percolate a while.

Let's explore the issue of "difference of degree" and "difference of kind." This seems like a promising way for us to go, since you favor the former in our thinking about God and man, and since you thereby reinforce my concern that your God is too finite, too little God-like, too much an enlarged human being.

First of all, do we agree that there is a difference of kind, and no mere difference of degree, between human persons and the most closely related non-personal animals? You mentioned things in your last message that would seem to imply a difference of kind, such as moral freedom. By saying difference of kind I mean that no gradual intensification or gradual refinement of animal instincts and animal desiring could ever turn into that freedom of persons by which they (persons) become morally good or bad. It follows that, when human persons and animals seem to be most alike, as when we speak of an animal "wanting" to do something, there is only an analogy between the animal's wanting and the person's exercise of free will. Between things different in kind, the similarities can be only analogical. I wonder if we are in agreement up to this point?

In your last message I understood you to say that with respect to time consciousness there is strict (non-analogical) similarity between persons and animals. But I think that the way in which the animal seems to live entirely in the present moment, when compared to the way in which a person can be burdened by the past, or unsettled by anticipating the future, as by anticipating one's death, makes for a difference in kind with respect to time consciousness. Just consider the need to interpret our past, the need to understand our past as more than a series of episodes, as Norris Clarke used to say, or the need to dissociate ourselves from something in the past by repentance: surely these suggest a time consciousness that is of a different order altogether from animal time consciousness. But this issue is perhaps secondary to the issue of a difference in kind between persons and animals; if we are agreed on that more fundamental difference in kind, we can leave for later the question of time consciousness.

Now I ask you: if there is a difference of kind between ourselves and the animals, would we not expect there to be even more, radically more of a difference of kind between ourselves and God? Can anyone think that the difference between God and man is a mere difference of degree, while thinking that the difference between man and animal is a difference in kind?

Is it then surprising that I acknowledge only analogical similarities between God and man? You are worried that God and man may thereby become estranged from each other, but is this worry really justified in light of the closeness, familiarity, affection, devotion that characterizes man in relation to certain animals? Would the closeness, familiarity, and affection be any greater if we talked ourselves into a mere difference of degree between ourselves and the animals?

The difference in kind between man and animals would seem, then, to have two consequences for our thinking about the difference between man and God: we should expect a difference of kind here, but this need not interfere with anything we want to say about the unity of God and man.

We don't disagree about space and heaven and God in quite the way you think we do. I too think that there must be spatial extension in heaven, otherwise my faith in the resurrection of the body would make no sense. But I don't think that God is extended in space (although the God-man is). God is indeed omnipresent, His spirit "fills the world," "nothing is hidden from Him." But theologians have long distinguished this omnipresence from the entirely different thing of occupying space like a material body. The human mind, after all, can range over the length and breadth of the material universe, and be cognitively present to it, without thereby physically occupying all the space that it traverses.

A blessed Sunday to you and Monica. Let us remember to "hold each other up" in prayer.

Your devoted friend,
John

*   *   *   *   *   *   *   *   *   *   *   *

October 31, 2010
Dear John,

I've been holding back in order to finish reading two books about God. I knew that one was likely to affect me rather profoundly but wasn't sure which one it would be. The first was Gerald Schroeder's *God According to God,* the second Bede Griffiths' *A New Vision of Reality.* They couldn't be further apart. Before addressing explicitly the concerns you've raised above, I'll summarize what I got from these two thinkers. Each represents an extreme, and I fall somewhere in between. They have helped me find the words to clarify my position. At the very least you will see what I am not. So here goes.

Schroeder is a brilliant MIT-trained physicist, a Jew whose view of God rests on two apparently conflicting sources: the universe as it is, and the Torah. His God is the author of the universe and everything in it, especially including earth and the human race. Schroeder's God is decidedly less than omnipotent and omniscient. He does not know the future. He is benevolent in an unpredictable sort of way, regrets mistakes that he makes, learns new things as his creation unfolds, sometimes changes his mind as a result of new knowledge, welcomes an argument from us, but as a rule hides his face from us. He cares profoundly how we take care of each other, even more than how we care about Him. I'll let him speak for himself:

> The biblical God may enter the fray when nature and humanity strays too far from the intended teleological path. In general, however, the running of the universe is not a power play by God. We and the laws of nature, which are themselves creations of the Creator, have a major role in the scenario. The Bible recognizes that flaws exist in nature's designs. It even describes them. The God of the Bible expects us to fix them. That's what partnership is all about. Not only are we our brother's and sister's keeper, we are even God's keepers, as is God our Keeper.

In the scientific part of this book, by the way, Shroeder does a brilliant statistical analysis on the probability of earthlike planets existing anywhere in the universe. The figure he arrives at is roughly 10,000. That works out roughly to one such planet for every 10 million galaxies. And these are only possible planets. He implies that unless God intervenes and directs the evolutionary process, we are probably the only such planet in the universe, and the fact that there is even this one is utterly improbable. To think that a few months ago I was worried about earth's insignificance!

Griffiths is a Catholic monk and mystic, an Englishman who lived his last thirty years in India, and died in 1993. He believes that in deep meditation—once the mind is completely stilled—we go to a place where everything is gathered into the unity of the one Person, the cosmic Lord. Then in and through the cosmic Lord everything returns to the transcendent unity beyond conception. The ultimate is beyond conception altogether. It is totally ineffable. That is why we have to constantly remember that all the words we use to speak of this are only pointers to that which is totally beyond. The Absolute itself is beyond all human comprehension and we use words, images and concepts taken from everyday finite experience in order to direct our mind, our will and our heart towards the Infinite and to allow that Infinite to enter our lives and transform them.

He believes that the materialism of the present age is a dead end and that the only way to recover what we've lost is to rediscover the forgotten wisdom of the great religions of the world. But these religions, he says, have become "fossilized" and must give way to "a cosmic, universal religion . . . in which the essential values of Christian religion will be preserved in living relationship with the other religious traditions of the world. This is a task for the coming centuries as the present world order breaks down and a new world order emerges from the ashes of the old." If you have time, I recommend you read his biography *Beyond the Dark*. It is hard to say whether Griffiths is more remarkable for his brilliance or his holiness.

Where do I stand? Schroeder strikes me as excessively anthropomorphic and therefore unattractive. On the other hand, Griffiths' "ultimate" is too transcendent and unapproachable. I would anchor my God somewhere between these extremes. If God transcends personhood, even infinite, perfect personhood, then I don't know how to relate to Him. I think you would feel the same way. Perhaps we have been concentrating so exclusively on our differences that we have failed to see our similarities. What guides me in all this discussion is my need to conceptualize God in a way that allows me to utterly adore and delight in Him. In order to do this, I must understand Him up to a point. Do we agree here?

Now to your most recent challenge. I cannot say with any confidence that I agree with your latest argument for a difference in kind between God and ourselves. Even after reading Griffiths, whose view on the future of religion I share—even after wanting to agree with him and you—I keep coming back to my commitment to God's personhood. In my view we are both literally persons—as different as a raging hurricane from a humble zephyr, or a solar flare from a blow torch—but still members of the same species: wind and flame in those two instances, persons in ours. So I hold out for a difference in degree, and do so without apology to the God who deigned to make me in his image. As for animals—let's specify dogs—we have a lot in common with them. We don't share personhood, but we are both mammals.

With regard to spatial extension, I come back to an earlier claim that our immortal souls were not created out of nothing (ex nihilo), but out of the divine substance itself. We are tiny God-seeds. Were it not for the anesthetic effect of being encased in flesh, we would not know ourselves as different from Him. God's contraction of Himself in us is essential for there to be a soul. Many mystics has spoken this way, Origen being the first Christian I believe, and I humbly defer to them in a matter I know so little about from direct experience but intuitively am attracted to. Now if God does in fact spread Himself out in this way, then He exists in space in us.

It was good to hear from you at last, John. You don't have to apologize for tardiness. I know how busy you are. I'll be in Mobile December 7–14.

All the best to my dear old friend,
Stafford

* * * * * * * * * * *

December 18, 2010
Dear Stafford,

Here I am, at long last, now that I've reported my grades. I see from a recent message of yours that you spent the last week in Mobile. How was it back in our home town? How are Stephanie and Ellen and your mother doing?

You mentioned a time or two that we should not only stress our differences. I have no reason to want to neglect all that we share. You can see for yourself how eager I am to find common ground with the likes of William James. I took to stressing our differences because you seemed to me to want to present yourself as a kind of Christian, and as one who might in all integrity participate in the sacramental life of the church. Your real views seemed to me to diverge fundamentally from Christianity, and so from the beginning of our exchange I wanted to understand better the nature of this divergence. And I think I do now understand it better. If we can agree on what is Christian and what is not, and can call things by their proper names, then I will feel more at liberty to explore our common ground. I won't feel I am compromising myself by dwelling with you on all that we share.

Thanks for telling me about those two books, and sharing with me your reactions to them. Among the thoughts you expressed in your message this one jumped out at me: "We are tiny God-seeds. Were it not for the anesthetic effect of being encased in flesh, we would not know ourselves as different from Him. God's contraction of Himself in us is essential for there to be a soul." I react violently against this sentiment both on philosophical grounds and on Christian grounds. I cannot think of any metaphysical conception more opposed to true personalism, as I understand it, than the conception according to which the individuality—the incommunicable identity—of each person is an accident imposed from without on that which, considered in itself, is something vaster than an individual person. You seem to say that we are at bottom really and literally identical with God, and acquire an illusion ("anesthetic effect") of otherness by being "encased in flesh." Remove the fleshy principle of individuation, you seem to imply, and we are resolved back into God. The I-thou relation with God thus rests on a material accident; as soon as the encasement in flesh is removed there remains only a solitary divine spirit with no possibility of interpersonal communion. It seems to me that this whole train of thought depends on primitive analogies with material things, such as a body of water that can be distributed over many cupfuls of water, the sides of the cups providing a temporary principle of individuation for each separate amount of water. It also strikes me as a kind of revival of the doctrine of Averroes, who taught that the intellect in human beings is really one divine spirit, and that the plurality of human beings exists only at the level of bodies; an individual person can be said to have his own body, but not his own mind.

Here then is a personalist argument against any kind of pantheism (and I take the thought of those sentences of yours just quoted as expressing pantheism): in pantheism the individuality of finite persons will inevitably be interpreted as an external form imposed on some kind of divine mass; but such external individuality can never be the individuality of persons, who rather exist as radically, inalienably individual, incommunicable beings. Persons would sooner be annihilated than blended back into God, or into anything else. This is why creation from nothing, mysterious as it is, seems to me to be a mode of origin far more resepctful of personal individuality than the pantheistic mode that you propose.

I now understand better why you are so resistant to the idea of a difference in kind between the divine person and human persons (even though I agree with you that both are rightly called persons, and not just in a metaphorical way of speaking). If my personhood is a small portion of the divine personhood, then God and I are persons in exactly the same sense, the difference between us being hardly more than quantitative. And there is something else in your recent messages that now makes more sense: the dispersal of God throughout space. This point of yours makes eminent pantheistic sense. Am I right in thinking that your thought in those sentences lies at the root of much of your religious thought, and also at the root of various points of disagreement between us?

In saying this I may seem to be taking back something I affirmed in an earlier message as a point of agreement between us. I said that we human beings are in some way "of the same stock" as God, and that this makes for a certain "consanguinity" with God that can be deeply felt in prayer and that somehow coheres with our sense of the divine otherness and transcendence. But there is no need to explicate this consanguinity in terms of a pantheistic oneness. Just consider our primary experience of consanguinity; it is what we experience with our parents and our children. There is nothing in this parental oneness that tends to compromise the incommunicability of me, my parents, or my children. In no way do I have to think that our familial oneness goes back to a oneness that preceded our existing as distinct persons, or that our existing as distinct persons is an "anesthetic effect," or that at the deepest level we are not really distinct persons at all. In the same way our being descended from God, our being related to Him, does not call for anything like the pantheistic account.

By the way, are there not major Hindu philosophers who agree with me? Didn't you years ago show me some passages in Madhva in which he argues for an irreducible plurality of finite persons?

I have the sense that this pantheism issue is as important as anything we have discussed in our exchange.

Blessings on you and Monica in the Advent season.

Your devoted friend,
John

*   *   *   *   *   *   *   *   *   *   *   *

December 19, 2010
Dear John,

Stephanie and Ellen are doing exceptionally well, and my mother is fading, though she still knows us all and has her personality fairly intact. She is not like—not yet anyway—your dear old Granny in her last years. I just pray that Mom passes soon and spares herself and all of us the horror of a broken brain.

Now to your latest. I want to hasten to defend the view you term pantheism. You write:

> I cannot think of any metaphysical conception more opposed to true personalism, as I understand it, than the conception according to which the individuality—the incommunicable identity—of each person is an accident imposed from without on that which, considered in itself, is something vaster than an individual person. You seem to say that we are at bottom really and literally identical with God, and acquire an illusion ('anesthetic effect') of otherness by being 'encased in flesh'. Remove the fleshy principle of individuation, you seem to imply, and we are resolved back into God. The I-thou relation with God thus rests on a material accident; as soon as the encasement in flesh is removed there remains only a solitary divine spirit with no possibility of interpersonal communion.

Let me try to make clear my point with a different analogy. When we procreate, we do it with a tiny cell we call a sperm. It comes out of our very substance. It is physical in nature, but when it fertilizes the egg, a tiny person is born. Where does that person come from? And what is its nature? Did it spring forth from nothing, or did it pre-exist? If it pre-existed, where was it to be found, and what was its nature? Now I know of no one who can bring forth something out of nothing. The most brilliant inventer is no better equipped to do such a thing than the lowliest street dog. If God can do such a thing, we have never had a hint of how He might go about it. To me it seems more plausible to assume He brings forth souls out of Himself, out of something already existing—a process we see happening around us all the time.

If that is so, does the possibility of an I-Thou relation vanish? As I view the matter, the tiny divine splinter that becomes us is a permanent gift, never to be taken back. Smothered in flesh, a substance deeply alien to its native splendor, the tiny soul struggles to express itself through its dense covering. And that struggle, the way we undertake it, is what defines our character and shapes our destiny. Is God vicious because He places us in such unwieldy bodies of dense flesh? Not as I see it. Anything less dense would have resulted in a natural absorption of the individual spirit back into the Great Spirit that is God, and that event would have nullified God's desire, which is to multiply his joy infinitely, soul by soul, person by person, in an ever-evolving relationship with Him.

At this point you challenge me with the following statement: "If my personhood is a small portion of the divine personhood, then God and I are persons in exactly the same sense, the difference between us being hardly more than quantitative." My reply is that quantitative differences usually lead to qualitative ones. The little one-dollar gold piece in my old coin collection was made out of the same gold as all the gold in Fort Knox, but no one would claim that it was even one-trillionth as valuable, especially when taking into consideration the tarnished condition of that coin caused by my careless concern for it. So my relation to God might be just like the tarnished little gold coin when measured against the pristine gold at Fort Knox.

Further, if it is true that my soul is of the same nature as God, that makes it all the more likely that we could develop a personal relationship. Whom do we care most about if not our own children? God cares so much about us because we are not only persons, but his very own children. And properly grateful children care so much about Him because He is their parent. I take the phrase "children of God" literally and thrill to its ring.

You are correct about Madhva. His commitment to God's transcendence was absolute. Yet he spoke of God as our antaryamin, or "inner controller," but not to the extent of nullifying our free will. A better translation might be "inner animator." Another great Hindu philosopher, Ramanjua, believed that the universe, including all matter and all souls, both animal and human, formed God's body—and he meant this literally. Just as we, our souls, control our bodies from within, so God controls the universe from within, though, again, not to the extent that He nullifies our free will. Ramanuja is not a pantheist, for God's inner life and his power are unique to Him. Yet He indwells all creation. (Sometimes Ramanuja is referred to as a "panentheist.") What is especially interesting about Ramanuja is his claim that the bliss of the liberated soul is identical in quality to the bliss of God Himself, yet there is eternally a distinction between the Lord and the soul: God is always the supreme Lord, the soul always the adoring creature. In the last analysis, though I share much with both Madhva and Ramanuja, I finally part company with them.

So does my position leave me outside the Christian fold? I don't think Jesus would part company with me because of my theology. He would if I didn't try to love God with my whole heart and try to love my neighbor as myself. On the other hand, the fathers of orthodoxy, as defined by Nicaea, Ephesus, and Chalcedon, probably would. And if they did, I think they probably get a stiff reprimand after crossing the great divide.

Stafford

*   *   *   *   *   *   *   *   *   *   *

January 3, 2011
Dear Stafford

Birthday blessings to you! I remember well celebrating it with you and Monica and Ellen in Mobile a few years back, and I would have liked to celebrate you in person this year too. In any case, I always remember you with special gratitude for your existence and for being in my life in the way you are.

Here is a kind a birthday present for you. I heard at a funeral a few weeks ago a melody from Finlandia by Sibelius. It was set to a religious text and worked very well in the funeral mass. Go listen to Finlandia on You-tube; it's only about 8 minutes long. I'm sure you'll find right away the exquisite melody I'm talking about. I can't hear it without being deeply moved. It may move you in the same way.

It is good, don't you think, to leave aside all words and propositions for once, and to share some music, as we did so often in the past.

As a related birthday present I'm attaching a beautiful meditation of Newman on the mystery of music.

> Let us take another instance, of an outward and earthly form, or economy, under which great wonders unknown seem to be typified; I mean musical sounds, as they are exhibited most perfectly in instrumental harmony. There are seven notes in the scale; make them fourteen; yet what a slender outfit for so vast an enterprise! What science brings so much out of so little! Out of what poor elements does some great master in it create his new world! ...is it possible that that inexhaustible evolution and disposition of notes, so rich yet so simple, so intricate yet so regulated, so various yet so majestic, should be a mere sound, which is gone and perishes? Can it be that those mysterious stirrings of heart, and keen emotions, and strange yearnings after we know not what, and awful impressions from we know not whence, should be wrought in us by what is unsubstantial, and comes and goes, and begins and ends in itself? It is not so; it cannot be. No; they have escaped from some higher sphere; they are the outpourings of eternal harmony in the medium of created sound; they are echoes from our Home; they are the voice of Angels, or the Magnificat of Saints, or the living laws of Divine Governance, or the Divine Attributes; something are they besides themselves, which we cannot compass, which we cannot utter,*though mortal man, and he perhaps not otherwise distinguished above his fellows, has the gift of eliciting them.

John

* * * * * * * * * *

January 28, 2011
Dear John,

I want to return to something you said in your last-but-one message. To my claim that we would not exist if God did not allow Himself to be contracted, you wrote:

> I react violently against this sentiment both on philosophical grounds and on Christian grounds. I cannot think of any metaphysical conception more opposed to true personalism, as I understand it, than the conception according to which the individuality—the incommunicable identity—of each person is an accident imposed from without on that which, considered in itself, is something vaster than an individual person. You seem to say that we are at bottom really and literally identical with God, and acquire an illusion ('anesthetic effect') of otherness by being 'encased in flesh.' Remove the fleshy principle of individuation, you seem to imply, and we are resolved back into God. The I-thou relation with God thus rests on a material accident; as soon as the encasement in flesh is removed there remains only a solitary divine spirit with no possibility of interpersonal communion.

At bottom the difference between us centers on where the soul comes from. Does it come from the primordial divine Consciousness or does it come from nothing? To me the former seems much more likely. But then I ask myself how the soul arises from such Consciousness, and the best I can do is to think of God as giving us a tiny sliver of Himself—not on loan, but for keeps. Far from seeing this as an insult to our personhood, I see it as a high compliment. It tells me that at the deepest level our life is divine—as divine as the great mystics of the world's religions have often claimed. Our divine pedigree doesn't mean, of course, that we exist on God's scale. We are far too small for that! But we are not so small that we know nothing of the divine life. I think that as we evolve over eons of future time we will know more and more of that life. But I do not anticipate being resolved back into the great "mass of consciousness" that we came from.

That would defeat the whole purpose of God's creating us—which is to multiply his joy and knowledge to the greatest extent possible, worlds without end. In pantheism such a gift would be sublated at some point, and our soul would resolve itself back into the Source. As I see it, the gift of individual personhood is forever.

I grant that our creation has an accidental quality to it: I came into being when my parents mated, or perhaps when my ur-parents mated a long time ago. But that would have to be the case in your theology as well. So how is my view of origins less personal than yours? Or do you think God had us specifically in mind from all eternity? That I think unlikely. I believe that my relationship with God developed, or at least had a chance to develop, once I was formed—by the accident of my parents marrying and mating. To say that God must have had us in mind before we came into being is unnecessary to personhood and seems to me a rather grandiose claim. What is important to me is that if I want to develop a relationship now, I can. Or I can go solo (foolishly I believe) like my atheist friends; it's up to me.

You take exception to my idea of contraction and consider it un-Christian. Yet we have the example of Jesus' contraction. If God can be contracted into a man once, He can do it again. Even the Creed says Jesus was fully man. So such a thing would seem to be possible on your terms. I trust that God in his goodness would not resolve me back into the divine stuff that I once was, thereby costing me my life as an individual. In my view, the very reason for incarcerating us in flesh was to make it possible for us— our tiny sliver of spirit—to cut away from our Creator Parent. Without matter to keep us apart, we would have been drawn back to the Source like a sun into a Black Hole. Our bodies wall us in until the time that we can emancipate ourselves from them and stand alone spirit to Spirit—or soul to God. This explanation of origins would also, incidentally, help to account for the evils that come to us as embodied beings. Matter blocks out, or partly eclipses, the divine splendor that in essence we are.

You will say that I am relying on "primitive analogies with material things," and of course I am. But the theory of *creatio ex nihilo* doesn't even have that to recommend it. We have never witnessed anything remotely like it—except at a magic show. Perhaps a magician's trick provided the source for such an odd conception. I am not saying that creation from nothing is impossible, like "the son of a barren woman," only that we have no analogy for it. In any case, I don't think there is anything essentially Christian about such a theory. As far as I can make out, it has no bearing on Christian piety—or any other kind of piety.

Are you sure that my scenario of how we came into being is essentially un-Christian? Or is it just unfamiliar? Of course, any theory of origins will seem absurd at first blush to an outsider. Such speculation is inherently risky. I am well aware that I have almost certainly missed something fundamental. But so, I strongly suspect, did Aquinas.

As always, I await with great anticipation your response. Remember: I don't want to win this debate nearly as much as I want us to mutually break through to some kind of wonderful accord. Which of us would have to give way the most is yet to be determined. As for the real "winner," it would be he who was won over to the new, and greater, truth—the one who changed the most.

Stafford

* * * * * * * * * * *

February 20, 2011
Dear Stafford,

I hope you got my birthday greetings. I trust you are in good health. I am too, except for an elevated blood pressure that needs medication, some hearing loss and ringing in the ears, and arthritic stiffness in the knees. As far as I know, dementia has not yet set in, but Pia may see it differently.

If I understand you correctly, you want to say that God fashions each human being out of His own substance. This seems to you to avoid the obscurity that lies in the concept of God creating out of nothing, and at the same time seems to you to be especially intelligible because God bringing forth creatures is now seen to be similar to something that is well known to us, namely to human parents bringing forth offspring.

My concern is to think of persons in a manner that respects the individuality that they have as persons. I argue that the blending and dividing that is possible with homogeneous material substances like water makes no sense with persons. Out of one mass of water several smaller masses can be formed, and these several can be poured back into the original mass. The individuality that is proper to the smaller masses is clearly an extrinsic and accidental individuality. But several persons cannot be fused together, nor can one person be broken into several persons. Several centers of freedom cannot be blended into one center of freedom, nor can one center of freedom be broken into several. The ontology of individuality is entirely different with persons than with homogeneous material substances. Individuality is intrinsic to a person in such a sense that the individuality cannot be taken away without the person being annihilated; there is no person-stuff that remains after the removal of individuality and is available for incorporation into a new person. In other words, there is a composition of "stuff" and "shape" that may describe the individuality of material things but is entirely irrelevant to individual persons.

Now any theology of the coming into being of human persons that cannot be separated from the stuff-shape paradigm has got to be a false theology, because as I see it the paradigm is false (when applied to persons). But your theology of the origin of human persons seems to be wedded to this paradigm. For you suppose that matter acts on the divine substance in such a way as to contract and to individuate a little piece of it, the result being a human person sprung from the divine substance. But this implies that once that matter is removed, the spirit of the human being is absorbed back into God. But this is nothing other than the stuff-shape paradigm, it is extrinsic individuality, it is degrading human persons to the status of parts of God, it is everything that is foreign to the ontology of individual persons. If we really exist as persons, then we must derive from God in some other way.

I see only two possibilities that respect the individuality of persons: either God creates us out of nothing, or we have always existed as persons. So either the Christian view or the Platonic view.

As I understand your pantheistic view of how we derive from God, it is not as close to human procreation as you suppose. For when I generate a child, that child as person is not a piece of me as person; the child is not held in being as a person separate from me by its matter, and it does not resolve itself back into me if it dies before I die. There is indeed a blending of sperm and egg at conception but this is not a blending of the parents as persons. The thing that troubles me in your pantheistic account of our derivation from God is not implied in the facts of human procreation, for these do not imply that the offspring arises as person from a "contraction" of the parental persons.

What follows from our difference on the ontogenesis of persons? Is our difference just a subtle theological difference, or is it also an existential difference? According to your view we are literally divine just as God is divine; this seems to follow from the fact that each of us exists as a certain contraction of God's substance. On the Christian view we are creatures of God, existing indeed in His image, participating indeed in His divinity, inhabited indeed by the Spirit, but not existing as literally divine. When the Creed says "one in being with the Father" it expresses what can hold only for the Son but not for each finite person. With this our difference seems to me to become an existential difference: the pantheist has a certain sense of himself as divine, as God, and the Christian has an entirely different sense of himself as creature under God.

I also wonder if your view does not tend to turn our relation to God into a monologue of God with Himself? If God is related to a human person as to a part of Himself, as to a "contraction" of Himself, is He not in the end dealing with Himself in dealing with that person? Contemporary religious thinkers like Levinas and Zizioulas lay great stress on the otherness of human persons. They say that this personal otherness needs to be recognized if a dialogue is not going to lapse into a monologue. The Christian account of how human persons derive from God seems to me to do justice to this otherness, whereas your pantheistic view seems to put the otherness into question (just like the otherness of creatures is put into question in the Hegelian theology).

As for what is Christian and what is not, I don't doubt that Jesus would welcome any honest searcher like yourself. But the question is whether there is anything like pantheism in His teaching as we have it in the New Testament. If you put together all that he says about His relation to His Father, and compare this with what He says about the relation to the Father that He offers His followers, you might well conclude that, though He didn't teach at the theoretical level at which you and I are talking, He held the creaturehood of human persons in a non-pantheistic sense. For instance, He never says to the apostles, "You and the Father are one," in the sense in which He says this of Himself. Thus if you had said to Jesus, "I and the Father am one," He would have contradicted you, and would have given you to understand that you can be His follower only by acknowledging your creaturely sonship in relation to the Father. The question we are discussing, then, has consequences for who is really a Christian. Christian discipleship is not achieved simply by, say, admiring the parable of the Good Samaritan; it is intimately connected with the issues we have been discussing.

In friendship,
John

*   *   *   *   *   *   *   *   *   *   *

February 26, 2011
Dear John,

I regard this message as the clearest and most powerful you've written to date. It is really very brilliant. If I weren't so wedded to the intuition that something coming from nothing is an oxymoron, I would be happy to concede.

The gist of your argument follows:

> . . . you suppose that matter acts on the divine substance in such a way as to contract and to individuate a little piece of it, the result being a human person sprung from the divine substance. But this implies that once that matter is removed, the spirit of the human being is absorbed back into God. But this is nothing other than the stuff-shape paradigm, it is extrinsic individuality, it is degrading human persons to the status of parts of God, it is everything that is foreign to the ontology of individual persons. If we really exist as persons, then we must derive from God in some other way.

I will now try to show you, by way of analogy, another way of looking at this. Consider the sun. Imagine it, however, not as pouring out its light upon an open system of planets, moons, and asteroids, but as completely surrounded by an immense integument of matter far distant from its center. And carved into that skin are tiny windows, trillions of them, that allow the sun's light to stream through. On the other side of this divine integument are innumerable worlds that the light lights up. Now the sun is God, the light pouring through a particular window is a particular soul, the window is the soul's senses and mind, and the world that greets the soul is some aspect of our physical universe.

I anticipate your objection, and it is a good one. You will wonder how my analogy accounts for the difference between God, the Source of light, and the soul. It does so in the following way. Most of the sun's energy burns inside and lights itself; we are only that part of it that escapes the center. We are far removed from the center, but we are nonetheless sunlight. We are sunlight that escapes the center and that reveals the tiny portion of the world that is our lot, our playground, our task. You look out your window, and I look out mine. You see only that which can be seen through yours, and I only that which can be seen through mine. We can compare what we see, but we cannot switch windows. A few of us when we meditate or pray fervently can look back toward the Source, but most of us are transfixed by the spectacle outside our window.

Again I anticipate your objection. "How does the ray of light that you are, become differentiated from the central Source?" At the beginning, only by its proximity to the window, is my answer. But I do not feel degraded by this analysis. Why should I feel degraded by being a "part of God"? On the contrary, I feel exalted. God burns and glows a zillion times brighter than I, but the substance that burns incandescently and immeasurably in Him is the same that burns dimly and minutely in me. Why dimly? Because I am so distant from the Center. Why minutely? Because my window is so tiny.

Again you will object: "But what accounts for the boundary that separates Him from you?" And the answer is: "The habit of looking out my window." It is that, and that alone, that separates us from God and you from me, at least at the beginning. Even if we were to lose all contact with our window and turn wholly, and forever, back in the direction of God, we would still retain our identity. For we would have welded the habit of being an individual into the little patch of God that we are. In fact, the only reason in the first place that God enclosed Himself with the universal integument with all its tiny openings was to create individuals. Needless to say,

He looks forward to the time that we grow tired of the process of individuation—because we have secured it so completely—and look back to him, the Source, with greater regularity. Archangels have been looking back for a long time, and that is why they are so much brighter than we are. They are closer to the Center and radiate with a brilliance and joy that we as yet know nothing of.

Again you will object that when it comes to making persons, one center of freedom, God, cannot be broken up into other centers of freedom, ourselves. That kind of thinking, you will say, applies only to physical substances, not to persons. And to that I say, Why not? How do you know? How can you be sure that you understand the powers of God when it comes to person-making? Of course, the process is acutely mysterious to us, but no more so than making persons from nothing.

But this I will grant you, and for this I am especially grateful to you— for I didn't see it with such clarity before. Your answer is more consistent with Christianity, and mine with the Hindu Vedanta. As you put it, "Christians will feel themselves to be 'under the judgment of God' in a sense in which people who think that they are literally divine cannot experience this." There is a little truth in this. For I feel under the judgment of something like a law of karma, which works more impersonally than the kind of judgment you have in mind. I feel a very real concern about my future after death, and I have every confidence that a virtuous life pays dividends in the world to come. Such a life will bring me farther away form my window and closer to the Center. And that is something I very much want! So I think we may be making a distinction without much difference, especially when we remember that the law of karma I speak of is ultimately under the administration of God. Nevertheless, you have a point.

Having granted this slight difference, however, it seems to me that whether we are Christian or Vedantic in our theory of person-making would be of very little consequence to God and would have little if any impact on how we live our lives. The important thing is that we see God as the Person-Maker. He, the Supreme Person, delights in making persons because he is a person himself. And persons are the noblest and highest form of being in the universe.

Stafford

PS I have been remiss in not telling you of my mother's passing about two weeks ago. She was at last freed from her old failing body, to the relief of herself and all who love her.

Now we are both the senior member of our families. No one to look up to—except Heaven.

* * * * * * * * * * *

March 16, 2011
Dear Stafford,

Many thanks for your last. I sense how hard you are trying to do me justice, and to anticipate my responses to your proposal. I appreciate the fact that you take my position very seriously, and I hope I am reciprocating in my stance to your position.

You make a valiant effort to clarify your position with a new analogy. In this analogy the "principle of individuation" of created persons is the window through which the divine light passes; sometimes you say it is the act of looking through the window out into the universe. If a created person looks back too soon at the divine source of light, then he or she is vulnerable, you say, to being absorbed into this divine source and to being deprived of his or her individuality. But if a created person keeps looking through his or her window, then the individuality of this person gets set in stone, so to say, and can no longer be lost even when the person turns back to God. My question to you is, how do you know that the individuality of a person lasts even in the absence of the individuating factor of the window? By assuming this you get indeed the desired conclusion, but does it make metaphysical sense? For if we think of some typical cases of material individuation, we find that the individuality that is imparted has no tendency to remain in the absence of constant support by the principle of individuation. For instance, a mass of water, individuated by the walls of a container, does not tend to hold together as one mass even when the walls are removed; let the walls hold a water mass together for eons, the water still flows back into a larger water mass, losing all its individuality, as soon as the walls are removed. This would mean that the individual created person, in your analogy, may be resolved back into God as soon as he turns away from his individuating window and looks back to God.

My question to you is just like the question that is asked of the Thomists when they affirm the survival of the individual person after death. They are asked how they know that the "separated soul" remains an individual, seeing that its principle of individuation is said in their system to be the matter of the body. It would seem that with the dissolution of the body the very thing that individuates is removed, hence leaving the soul without any way of enduring as an individual. I've never heard a convincing Thomistic answer to this question. To defend your position I think you will have to succeed where they have failed; you will have to show how an extrinsic principle of individuation (as your window-analogy undoubtedly is) can lead to the intrinsic individuality of persons that lasts even in the absence of the action of the principle.

Notice that it won't do to say that God won't allow individual persons to be dissolved when they turn back to Himself; the point is that in the nature of things the individuality of these persons may not be able to endure apart from the constant activity of the individuating principle. You would enter a voluntaristic universe with all kinds of unwanted consequences if you let God annul the nature of things whenever He wants to get some desired result. If you invoke "mystery" for this kind of divine arbitrariness, you would have basically given up on philosophy as a way of thinking about God.

Another difficulty in your analogy arises when we consider that an individual human person can turn against God, can revolt against God, can want to dethrone God and to usurp His place. How is this possible in a being who supposedly exists as a contraction of the divine radiance, who therefore is ontologically divine? How can a divine being become hostile to the divine? How can God turn upon Himself in hatred?

Created persons seem to need more freedom from God than they have in your analogy, if they are to be capable to rising up against God. But if we think of these persons as created by God in the Christian sense, then they have enough independence in being to exercise their freedom against God. It is remarkable that the Christian idea of creation out of nothing, which seems to involve so radical a dependency on God, in fact opens up a space between God and the created person that lets the created person exist in a greater independence of being than he can possibly have in the setting of your pantheistic light-analogy. I hold that in order to exist as person a creature needs just this greater independence of being.

A further difficulty I see in your light-analogy is based on our experience of encountering God in prayer. According to your light-analogy this encounter tends to dissolve our individuality. It diverts us away from the principle of our individuation. It would in fact dissolve our individuality if each individual person had not already, as you say, accumulated a measure of individuality by looking through its window. This accumulated individuality seems to you to be a kind of bulwark against the de-individualizing effect of turning back to God. But many believers would say in response to you that the experience of encountering God in prayer has a profoundly individuating effect on us. If Newman has correctly described the encounter with God in conscience in *The Grammar of Assent,* ch. 5, sec. 1, then when in the inner sanctum of conscience we are pierced with a sense of a divine judgment on our choices, we "quicken" in our selfhood, in our sense of existing as a distinct person. Far from blending into the God who makes Himself felt in conscience, we experience radically our non-identity with Him, for we experience our being under His judgment and being answerable to Him. One goes forth from such encounters with a greatly enhanced sense of one's personal incommunicability. This means that the facts of religious experience are just the opposite of what your light-analogy leads us to expect.

At this point I should come back to the idea of creation out of nothing. It is the alternative that I have offered to your pantheistic view of finite persons, and yet it is a notion that seems to you unsupported by anything in our experience. Let me try to find in our experience something like a creation out of nothing.

I assume that on the question of free will we agree in setting aside all compatibilist accounts of free will and that we agree in affirming a libertarian account of it, that is, agree in affirming a freedom of will that falls outside of, or transcends, all determinism. Now I ask if a truly free act does not involve a certain creation out of nothing. Is it not something radically new in relation to all that has gone before in the world, just like a person who is created out of nothing is radically new and is not just a "new edition" of existing materials? Of course, performing a free act is a far cry from creating a person out of nothing, but there may be in the free act enough of a "creating out of nothing" to connect the divine activity of creating persons with something known to us in experience, and thus to render it conceivable. What do you think? Is there something here worth pursuing?

In friendship,
John

*   *   *   *   *   *   *   *   *   *   *

April 4, 2011
Dear John,

You understand my position very well, and I am grateful for that. I see your contesting of my window analogy with the counter-analogy of the water container as a legitimate move to make, but it is far from decisive. For the water has no internal principle keeping it intact as a unit once the walls of the container are withdrawn. If we must use an analogy from the purely physical world, then a magnet would be more appropriate. When in the presence of a magnet, iron filings cling to the magnet and cling to each other. Think of the soul's character, the fruit of countless free choices, as a kind of internal magnet holding the soul together and keeping it intact. The window would be merely the means of getting the new individual—the soul—started. In time it would be capable of holding together on its own, even in the absence of the window. Thus the last of your concerns—that the soul when looking away from its window would collapse back into the undifferentiated divine substance—would be met. This entire individuating process would, of course, take place under divine direction. It would be the way God goes about creating new souls. Something radically new evolves, but it began as something, not nothing.

There is an easy solution to the Thomistic dilemma that you mention, and I'm surprised to hear that no Christian philosopher has thought of it. After all, it is St. Paul himself who speaks of a spiritual body after death. Irrespective of St. Paul, there is a tremendous amount of testimony coming from spiritualist sources, as well as earlier Stoic, Hindu, and Buddhist sources, that incarnate beings like ourselves have several layers of subtler bodies underneath our grosser physical body, and that at death they remain intact and even become the soul's "outer" body in the etheric or "astral" realms that make up the afterlife environment. Nowadays these subtler bodies are often referred to as the "astral body." So there is no difficulty accounting for a continuing individuality after death: The astral body keeps the soul from slipping back into an undifferentiated state. In fact, we could even do away with the window analogy as a means of accounting for the soul's individuation. It may be that the Divine simply encases a tiny part of his being in a material body, both gross and subtle, to bring to birth each new soul, and that the soul is never without some sort of body throughout its entire existence.

The challenge you bring to me concerning the soul's rebellion needs special handling, and I am grateful for this challenge. First let me say that I entirely agree with you that free will is a fact of our lives and that com-patibilist arguments are deceptive and must be rejected. But I also want to make it clear that I view God as free, too. God in my view is entirely capable of committing evil—though let us hope He never does. Now when we finite beings do evil, we are not doing something that our divine birthright rules out. What differentiates us from God is our finiteness. The fact of our being encased in matter makes it harder—much, much harder—to choose the nobler, more difficult course when confronted with a temptation. So our embodiment accomplishes two goals. Not only is it crucial in the individuating process; it is crucial to the ennobling process as well. For without the moral challenges made possible by our finiteness, we would not be moral beings. We might be happy lotus eaters, but we would not bring the kind of value to the universe that God intended—namely good-ness.

It isn't often that I disagree with Newman when he speaks as a man of spirit, but his analysis of what happens during moments of deep prayer might owe more to his theology than the naked experience of prayer. The world's greatest mystics, those adepts at deeply communicating with the Divine—including many Christians—describe the climax of their experience as one of uniting with the Divine, sometimes even to the point of a seeming identification. Over and over they describe a sense of transcending their narrow individualities and merging with the Divine. This way of speaking is entirely consistent with the divine ontology presented here. What keeps the soul of the mystic intact is not its desire, but its encasement in the body, both gross and subtle, which renders the soul's nostalgic desire for a complete, irrevocable merger an impossibility. Newman, by contrast, is describing an experience known to both of us. I think you would agree that every deep, sharply focused experience quickens our selfhood. Deep prayer is one such experience. At the risk of sounding paradoxical, I think that the mystic's crowning experience of unity with the Divine also quickens her experience of the being she is—not during the experience, but after she comes down and contemplates her extraordinary blessedness. So I don't think it is her sense of individuality that is quickened, but her sense of gratitude when considering her blessedness.

In your last paragraph you describe my view of the soul as a "new edition of existing materials," and therefore not as radically new as a being created out of nothing. You then compare this radical form of newness to the "truly free act" of a truly free agent. Like you, I esteem the ability that we free beings have; it is mysterious and rather awesome; it makes possible, as nothing else could, the creation of eternal value in God's universe. But the phrase "new edition of existing materials" demeans the soul that emerges from this amazing act of creation. The words "new edition" imply that there was once an older edition, and that is not what I have in view at all. Every new soul is genuinely new and unique; there was never an older edition of it. The fact of its being created out of the divine substance rather than out of nothing only enhances its ontic value. To put it another way, it's not the soul's newness that makes it greater when viewed in your way as opposed to my way—for on both accounts the soul is equally new—but the nature of the new thing that it is. And I cannot see why the soul's being made out of the divine substance makes it less worthy, or the divine creativity less momentous, than if it were made from nothing.

Stafford

*   *   *   *   *   *   *   *   *   *   *

June 8, 2011
Dear Stafford,

Let me start by recalling the larger issues that, as I understand it, we are pursuing. I find that we can get so absorbed in the question of whose analogies have which liabilities, that I at least can get a little disoriented about the larger issues that elicited the analogies in the first place.

From the beginning of our exchange I have been repeatedly surprised by the finitude of your God. When you make God spatially extended and therefore bodily, or when you speak of Him as unable to be present to all of His creation at the same time (you said in an earlier letter that in giving attention to one part of it He is diverted from other parts of it), you seem to describe a finite being, not the living God. In your last letter you greatly increased my sense of the finitude of your God, and the non-divinity of your god, when you said that this god can in principle do wrong and that we have to hope that he doesn't. You (like William James) seem to me to live in a world of larger and smaller finite beings, not in a world of finite beings under the infinite God. You also seem to me to rely on quantitative modes of thinking, and on what strikes me as naive "picture-thinking," to a degree that surprises me in a man of your philosophical education.

At the same time, the metaphysical "weakness" that I keep finding in your conception of God seems to get passed on to the human person; the human person is less than he really is when he is taken to be a mere part of any larger whole, and what I call your pantheism seems to push persons into the category of a part, especially your account of the origin of individual persons through a divine spark encased in a body. So my overall claim in these letters is this: if you let God be God, then the human person emerges much more clearly with the dignity proper to himself. Or rather my overall claim is more restricted: the Christian God is something very different from your finite god, and human persons have in a Christian setting a worth and dignity that they cannot have for you. I have always thought that we have a better chance of agreeing on what is and what is not distinctly Christian, than of agreeing on the substantive issues.

When I return to the last messages we have exchanged I notice a question that I should have raised earlier. It seems that your God is in the same position as we human beings: he too is a composition of matter and spirit. Perhaps this is behind your new claim, which greatly surprises me, that He can in principle do wrong; if you follow Plato in placing in matter our vulnerability to wrongdoing, then it follows that your material and spatially extended God can do wrong. In any case, I had been thinking of your position like this: the divine spirit encounters matter, and some spark or fragment of the divine spirit gets "encased" in matter, thus giving rise to a human person. But this way of thinking about it obscures the fact that the divine spirit is, on your view, in exactly the same composite condition that human persons are; material encasement is found in your god no less than in man. So one enmattered spirit gives rise to lesser enmattered spirits—do I have that right? I suppose in the end that you will rely on the analogy with human generation to explain the origin of human beings from god? But the more you rely on this analogy, the more you will feed my suspicion that for you God and man are of the same order, God being as finite as man, since after all generation occurs within the same species.

There is one point I recently raised that seems to me not to be understood by you as I meant it. My alternative account of the origin of human persons works with the Christian notion of creation out of nothing. This seems to me to preserve the sovereignty of God and to avoid thinking of human persons as parts of God. But you object that the idea is inconceivable, since there is nothing in our experience that helps us to understand creation out of nothing. It is at this point that I introduced human free choice, arguing that it involves a kind of creation out of nothing, that is, a radically new start that cannot be derived with necessity from anything that preceded the choice. Sometimes philosophers and theologians speak of a certain work of self-creation that we carry out by our free choices. Of course, it is not a self-creation whereby we put ourselves absolutely into being, but a self-creation at the level of actualizing ourselves. But there may be enough "creation out of nothing" even at the level of actualization, to enable the Christian "creation out of nothing" to make sense to us, and to enable us to make use of all the advantages that it has for the issues we are discussing.

As for God being able to do wrong, I think that with this claim you fall behind not just Christianity, but Plato too: see the end of Republic II, where the goodness of God is an essential necessity, not a contingency to be hoped for. You may ask what becomes of the freedom of God if we affirm His essential goodness. I would think that a significant divine freedom of choice remains when God chooses to create rather than not create, or to create this person rather than some other possible person, or to create just so many persons when He could create more, or to intervene in human affairs in this way rather than in that. His essential goodness does not dictate any of these divine actions carried out in the contingent world; they have an element of what I called earlier "inscrutable election." In this way we could think of God as exercising freedom of choice even while remaining intrinsically, necessarily good.

As for your new analogy with the magnet, with this you seem to me simply to describe the thing that is calling for explanation, with the description substituting for explanation. You start with the "anesthetic illusion of individuality," which is supposed to morph into real individuality. The task is to make the transition intelligible, not just to picture the transition happening. What does it mean at all for the illusion of individuality to coagulate into real individuality? Why does an illusion start to hold together like a magnet attracting filings? Why does the holding together effect a transition from illusion to reality?

There is one other point I raised that I think merits more of a response from you. I raised it in my message of Jan. 12 like this: "I also wonder if your view does not tend to turn our relation to God into a monologue of God with Himself? If God is related to a human person as to a part of Himself, as to a 'contraction' of Himself, is He not in the end dealing with Himself in dealing with that person?"

I became a grandfather on May 12: John Henry and his wife Robin had a little girl, Magdalene Marie. Thanks be to God!

In friendship,
John

*　*　*　*　*　*　*　*　*　*　*　*

June 11, 2011
Dear John,

From the beginning I have quietly rejected your naming of me as a pantheist. Now let me come out of the closet. I'm actually a panentheist. Panentheists affirm the immanence of God, but they hold onto his transcendence as well.

Now to some of the specifics of your last letter. Let's begin with the notion of God as being capable of doing wrong. It would be foolish of me to advance this point of view other than provisionally. But in trying to push personalism as far as it will go, it seems natural to draw on the human experience and see where it takes us. After all, we are the only persons we have any direct knowledge of. So, rather than say that God is essentially good in any strong sense—in the sense that He would be incapable of doing evil—I would prefer to say that God is essentially free to do as He pleases. Then I would take the next step, which is that just as there is a vast moral difference between a criminal and a saint, there is an even vaster difference between a saint and God. By that I mean that although a saint might have her heart set irrevocably on the good, she might occasionally lose patience or play favorites because she was exhausted or exasperated. God, on the other hand, would not know such limitations, and thus his natural tendency to do good—vast good, goodness on an unthinkable scale—would not be undercut. In other words, the good-prone heart of the saint and God would be identical, but the capacity to stay the course of goodness would be drastically different. Still, God being free, could theoretically do evil. If he couldn't, then whatever else you might say of Him, you couldn't call Him a Person. Freedom to do good or evil goes to the very core of what it means to be a person, whether finite or infinite. Would you agree?

I question the logic of your theology when you write that "human persons have in a Christian setting a worth and dignity that they cannot have for you" or that God is "in the end dealing with Himself" rather than independent persons. That, of course, would be true if I were really a pantheist. But panentheism allows plenty of scope for otherness. Let me say that I agree with Levinas and Zizioulas when they stress the otherness of persons. But does God's being present within or around me in some wondrous, inconspicuous manner detract from my otherness? I certainly don't feel very godly! Godliness is not my natural modus operandi! Whether we are made from nothingness or from something pre-existing in the divine fecundity—either way we are dealing with a process utterly inscrutable—we are as we are. We are obviously different from each other and different from our Maker, even though we are made in his image—whatever exactly that means. Can we agree on this?

You make a good point below when you reject my speculation that God might be incapable of being simultaneously aware of all that is going on everywhere in the universe. If God is truly the all-encompassing Spirit, then perhaps He can be with all of us and know all of us by name, wherever in the universe we may be—trillions of us on millions of planets! This idea is very attractive to me, and when I pray in the morning, I act as if I believe this to be so. Do I really? Not if God is purely transcendent. My panentheism, however, makes all this possible. And I act on it. In saying this I am admitting an earlier and rather embarrassing mistake. I was too intent on establishing a similarity between the Creator and the creature. I thank you for pushing me out of this commitment to what Emerson called a "foolish consistency."

I think you have misunderstood my position on God's materiality, or perhaps my position has shifted slightly. The early Stoics did not speak of the Logos as being encased in matter but as being matter. And by "being matter" they meant that God, or the Logos, was something rather than nothing. They had so exalted a conception of divine matter that there is no meaningful distinction that I can see between the pure spirit of Plato and the utterly ethereal matter of the Stoic's God. I find the religion of the early Stoics one of the best and noblest our planet has ever seen, and it had a profound impact on some of the best men of ancient Greece and Rome, from Zeno the Stoic down to Seneca. So the Logos wasn't encased in anything that served as a limiting principle. And that is the way I intended, or at least intend now, to regard the divine substance. The only reason I am inclined to side with the Stoics is that, as I said earlier, it makes it easier to deal with the challenges of materialists when they attack dualism over its inability to account for the interaction between soul and body: If the soul and the body are both material in some sense, even though the stuff from which the soul is made is radically less dense than the body's matter, then interaction can be better defended. But if it turns out that I am wrong, and God (and souls) are matterless after all, I would not be surprised. Nor would I be put out. Nor would I even feel I had made a mistake. Since the Divine Matter is not conceived by the Stoics as limiting God anymore than a purely immaterial substance, I see here a distinction without any meaningful difference.

I still find God's creating us out of nothing unappealing—note that I don't say illogical. In being committed to such a view you are, I think, doing all you can to protect God's radical otherness from us, his puny creatures. But isn't it possible you are going overboard? If we really are made in God's image, then is it really such a stretch to claim that we have a little divine DNA in our makeup? Please don't think I have some theory about how the creation actually occurs. The actual process must remain as mysterious as *ex nihilo* creation. As with the case in the paragraph above, I see this little spat as inconsequential. The important thing is to protect God's grandeur and awesomeness on the one hand and his nearness to us and even intimacy with us on the other. To me *ex nihilo* makes intimacy harder to come by, and the talk of sonship is harder to defend. In either case, I think it's unwarranted to claim that one or the other hypothesis is more Christian than the other.

Stafford

* * * * * * * * * * *

June 30, 2011
Dear Stafford,

One way in which we could continue this line of discussion would be to look together at a short but profound passage of Guardini that has strongly influenced me (in his book, *Person and World* [Chicago: Henry Regnery and Co., 1965], 14-32). It would bring a third voice in to our exchange, and let us go deeper into the meaning of Christian creation. I could send it to you. Or you may feel that the discussion has reached a certain completeness and can be brought to a conclusion. Tell me where you think we are and what our possibilities are.

John

* * * * * * * * * * *

July 4, 2011
Dear John,

I am delighted with the Guardini chapter you sent me. He offers wonderful insight into the seeds of human rebellion: the soul's need for autonomy before it can thrive and grow, and the natural, defensible resistance to living under the thumb of another. And then his concluding thoughts on the difference between human others and the Divine Other. Deep and wonderful reflections that I wish we could talk over while peering out over Salzburg or while walking along more familiar paths behind your old home in Mobile.

His discussion of autonomy strikes me as prescient. It is as if he foresaw what would happen in the West as God became more and more resented until he was finally snuffed out. How different our upbringing was. We were encouraged at every step to love and trust the Divine Other. We lived in a kind of cocoon, and the more docile among us (you and I) did not feel the need to rebel. How unlike our children! Our age's rebellion has become mindless and totally out of control: the good and necessary intuition toward autonomy has usurped every other consideration. Aristotle's mean has been missed.

Stafford

* * * * * * * * * * * *

July 7, 2011
Dear Stafford,

I was delighted to see you picking the very things out of Guardini that I have long admired in that passage! I am particularly taken by the idea that God releases created things into a "being of their own" and does not manipulate them like marionets. Very wise too is his warning that created things should not be taken so strongly as symbols of the divine as to be compromised in their "own being." It is really quite a bold thought of his that modern science captures here a certain truth about the world that easily gets lost in a highly religiously charged view of the world. But then he brings in the apparently contradictory idea that the creature is so radically grounded in the creator that it is almost dangerous to say that God is other than the creature. Another bold move of Guardini. The mystery and paradox of created being seems to me to emerge with unusual clarity and depth. Guardini is a deep thinker, and a personalist thinker. I feel deeply indebted to him and for that reason am very happy that we share an appreciation of him.

John

*   *   *   *   *   *   *   *   *   *   *

July 11, 2011
Dear John,

The theologian Marcus Borg—have you read him?—is also a panentheist, and in his book *The Heart of Christianity* he describes God in the following way:

> "God is the name we use for the nonmaterial stupendous, wondrous 'More' that includes the universe even as God transcends the universe. This is God as the 'encompassing Spirit,' the one in whom 'we live and move and have our being,' the one who is all around us and within us. God is the one in whom the universe is, even as God is more than the universe; the Mystery who is beyond all names, even as we name the sacred Mystery in our various ways."

Borg is very much a personalist, incidentally. He writes, "God has more the quality of a 'you' than an 'it,' more the quality of a person than the quality of an impersonal 'source.'"

Stafford

*   *   *   *   *   *   *   *   *   *   *

July 11, 2011
Dear Stafford,

Many thanks for the selections from Borg, which I read with interest. I have never read him, and I know only what you have showed me from his writings. What he calls "out there" supernaturalism seems to me very close to what is called deism. Recall how Guardini resists a supernaturalist dualism of God and the world by insisting that God is in a sense not other than the world. Recall too the Christian idea that Christians are incorporated into the God-man like limbs and organs of a body and like branches of a tree. That certainly puts God within man and man within God in a radical way. The question that arises for our exchange is this: is this idea of a mutual indwelling of God and man compatible with the idea of God creating the world out of nothing? Is there any logic leading from creation out of nothing to deistic supernaturalism? Is it perhaps the case that the immanence of God in the world is better explained on the basis of creation out of nothing (since the God who creates the world out of nothing must act continuously to preserve it in being)?

I understand why you prefer to be called a panentheist rather than a pantheist, andI will explain at the end what I mean by describing your position as pantheist.

As for God being able to do wrong, it may help to take note of the debate going on within analytic philosophy as to whether "being able to act otherwise" necessarily belongs to every exercise of freedom. Some say that it suffices for freedom that I originate an act as my own, and that I need not in all cases have the option to perform it or not to perform it. Thus we might say that if Mother Theresa had been asked to open an abortion clinic in one of her religious houses, she could only have said no; providing abortions would not have been a live option for her, could not have tempted her in the least. Her no was free because she originated it in herself, and owned it as person, not because she could as well have said yes. Could it then be that God is free in being good, not in the sense that He could do bad, but only in the sense that His will to be good originates exclusively in Him? His "inability" to do bad, based on the fact that He does not just have goodness but is Goodness, no more compromises His freedom than Mother Theresa's "inability" to provide abortions made her refusal unfree.

Of course, there are exercises of freedom that do require an option, and such freedom of choice is also found in God. Here we come back to the "election and gratuity" of which I spoke in earlier messages. God creates this world though He could have created another one, He creates these persons though He could have created different ones in their places, He creates them now though He could have created them later, etc. The contingency of the world goes back, I would hold, to such divine freedom of choice. I would just say that being good rather than bad is not the result of a divine choice; it is a free act of God, but not an act of free choice.

In the course of discussing this point you make another one of those statements of yours that seems to me to efface the most fundamental difference between God and creature. You say: *"the good-prone heart of the saint and God would be identical,* but the capacity to stay the course of goodness would be drastically different" (my italics). Christians, and surely not only Christians, want to say that our creaturely goodness is a participation in God's supreme goodness, that He empowers us to be good by letting us share in His own divine and superabundant goodness. But then it follows that the goodness of the divine source can hardly be "identical" with the creaturely participation. It can hardly be the case that our human goodness differs from the divine goodness only by the fact that it faces obstacles of execution that the divine goodness does not face. I think that the Christian idea of creation is just what you need as a bulwark against your tendency to put God and man on the same level; for creator and creature are not on the same level.

You write: "But does God's being present within or around me in some wondrous, inconspicuous manner detract from my otherness?" The thing in your thought that seems to detract from my otherness is not your affirmation of God "being present within and around me," but the fact that I am at my core a spark or sliver of God. This raises questions about me really being other than God, and also about me really belonging to a different order of being from God. Your tendency to put God and man on the same level may have one of its roots in your idea that I start out as identical with God.

I don't think it is a complete statement of my position to say that creation from nothing is important to me as a way to preserve the divine majesty; it is equally important for me as a way to give the created person the "space" of which Guardini speaks, the space it needs so as to come into its own being. Your own view-a sliver of God that somehow morphs into a new person-seems to me to hold the human person so fast to God as to put in jeopardy the space needed for living his or her own being. This is just my old concern about the otherness of the created person, put in different words.

In connection with the materiality of God, I think you may want to be more cautious about borrowing from the Stoics. The Stoic Logos is not any kind of personal God and is generally taken to be a species of pantheism. To view God as material is not surprising within the setting of pantheism. But if, as you insist, you do not want to be a pantheist, and if you affirm the transcendence of God along the lines of Borg, and if you recognize a personal God in a sense unknown to the Stoics, then the material God that sufficed for the Stoics may no longer suffice for you.

Let me return to my use of the term pantheism in describing your position. I fully acknowledge your intention to be a kind of panentheist. I am far from ascribing to you a pantheism like that of Spinoza (*deus sive natura*). If I persist in using this term for your position, know that I am referring 1) to your account of the origin of each human person as a part of God, and 2) to your (resultant) tendency to underestimate the fundamental difference between God and man, that is, to resist thinking of this difference in terms of creator and creature, and 3) to your borrowing from the Stoics the idea of the divine materiality, an idea that is hard to separate from the Stoic pantheism.

John

* * * * * * * * * * * *

July 25, 2011
Dear John,

I was delighted to see that your response to Borg was as positive as mine to Guardini. We are both panentheists.

I gladly accept your analogy to Mother Teresa and the abortion clinic (a hilarious example, incidentally). Yes, God's freedom to choose evil must be just like that. What a deep and mysterious sense of freedom that is: an act that is free but at the same time does not allow the possibility of acting in a manner that violates one's essential character: freedom that is, speaking metaphorically, horizontal but not vertical. A very deep thought that I wish we could tease out some more. Thanks for the clarification. I'm a little troubled, though, by what seems to open the door to predestination in us mortals, but probably we don't have to go there. It's enough to acknowledge that we mortals are simply free in both the vertical and horizontal sense, and that is one of the ways we differ fundamentally from God—though in time let us hope we can eliminate vertical freedom, the freedom to will the bad. In any case, that is certainly what you and I are working toward!

I appreciate your concern to wrest me from the coils of an incipient pantheism, but I don't feel as if I am caught up in those coils. I think that my account of the origins of the human soul is sufficiently nuanced to save it from the charge of denying the divine otherness, and that the Stoic's God is as personal as I would need Him to be. About this latter point I could be wrong, for I am no expert on Stoicism, but what I know of it up to this point strikes me as a full-blooded panentheism of the kind that Guardini and Borg urge on us. The only difference between Stoicism and Christianity lies in the materiality of the divine substance, and that strikes me as a very minor point once the Stoic's notion of the vast range of materiality is grasped. Plato had such a negative view of the material universe that he relegated it to the Cave, and all Christianity followed. I prefer a more graduated account of reality: a Great Chain of Being, with many, many gradations, wound round a single substance. I think very little hinges on our disagreement, incidentally. One view is no less likely to serve as incentive for saint-making than the other.

Now let me take the discussion in a different direction. The philosopher of religion Jacob Needleman writes in his latest book, *What is God?*:

> . . . how could the human race have ever dreamt that God could act in a merciful, just manner in the human world without the presence of individual men and women who have received the inward God of consciousness within their own human frame? That is the real unrecognized illusion about religion in our world—not the illusion of God's existence that Freud attempted to expose. The deeper, widespread illusion that God can and should act mercifully and justly in human history without the 'instrument ' of God-inhabited human beings.

He goes on to say that the idea of God intervening in human affairs "is defeated by the world we live in and which, no doubt, we have always lived in." From the countless genocides of the last hundred years to the afflictions of our own precious children, it is obvious that God does not intervene just because we earnestly want Him to and ask Him to. God expects us to solve our own problems. But this is no bleak prospect. Needleman continues:

> Wherever the process of cosmic creation is taking place [and he imagines innumerable earthlike planets spread throughout the cosmos], there is, and must be, a specifically human energy, filling, as it were, the stages and steps in the descent and manifestation of what it is that originally emanates from the Source. It is at these everywhere-appearing junctures in the cosmic and planetary world that Man is created and needed as the microcosmic God, the 'image and likeness of God', whose work it is to 'make straight the ways of the Lord.'

Let me add that Needleman is very much a personalist and panentheist, though he would not use those terms.

I'm not sure you will share the excitement that these words create in me—especially the idea that God does not intervene in human history but depends on us to intervene when justice and mercy are all but forgotten. Needleman takes a dim view of a supernatural deity who would sometimes jump in to solve our dilemmas when we ask Him to. It would demean and enfeeble us. Yet God is involved in our attempts. For it is his energy, his grace (to use traditional language), that rolls through us and makes us yearn for God and for God's ways. So he is involved—through us.

> What, after all, is the meaning of my own human life if I live without yearning for what the religions call God? What is the meaning of our lives if we cannot love, cannot be just, cannot hate only what is evil and cannot love only what is good? What is the meaning of our lives if we live enmeshed in the troubled sleep of fear, resentment, fantasy, cruelty, sentimental stupidity, or even the bloated, arrogant atheism that succumbs to the essence of the very illusions it has honorably sought to expose [he has in mind Hitchens, Harris, Dennett, and Dawkins]—

namely, the worship of a false god that has sought to usurp the place of the real God?

It would be predictable to ask at this point what the object of prayer might be if God does not intervene directly. You once said that when you pray you sit quietly and receive and feel his presence. That in my view is exactly what we should be doing when we pray. I call that kind of prayer meditation, and it is the highest form of prayer. But what about petitionary prayer? Why do it if God does not intervene from the outside? I can only defer to the wisdom of the Church in its insistence that our prayers are heard and acted on by the saints and angels who love us. In particular I address the guardian and guiding spirits who might be attached or assigned to me for some reason. How wise is the Church in telling children they have guardian angels. I take them more seriously now than ever I did as a child!

Stafford

* * * * * * * * * * *

August 6, 2011
Dear Stafford,

Many thanks for your last message, so full of your characteristic spirit of eager enthusiasm. How many times over the years has this spirit of yours lifted me out of the spiritual doldrums and communicated new energy to me.

I'll need to read more of Borg before I can tell whether I admire him as much as you admire Guardini.

I must admit I can't warm to the Needleman passage (for which I thank you).

His idea that God doesn't act to achieve justice, that we are the only ones who can achieve it, makes eminent atheist or pantheist sense. If there is no God personally distinct from us human persons, then of course there is no one there acting for justice apart from us human persons.

But if you and I are theists in a different and stronger sense, if we recognize a God who is personally distinct from us, who has His own power of acting, then the question of His acting in the world is not so easily settled. I think that it will often be true that, as you suggest, God doesn't intervene as we ask Him to intervene, because He wants us to do some growing, which is only possible if He keeps silent. But there is much in our religious traditions, and certainly in the Christian tradition, which encourages us to ask and to expect to receive. We needn't go beyond the "Our Father" to be reminded of this! This use of petitionary prayer seems to me to cohere with God as personal. So I don't think it would be right to take the "pedagogical reserve" of God—an undeniable reality, which we often fail to recognize—and to drive the idea so far that we end up denying any and every divine initiative in history and in our individual lives.

I suspect that this pedagogical reserve of God is the point that really interests you, and I don't see why we shouldn't explore it further together within the theistic framework that we share.

I was very pleased to see the growth towards faith in Louie's review of your book. As his godfather I take a particular interest in all that concerns his faith. I especially liked his disdain for the guild of professional philosophers and theologians!

In friendship,
John

*   *   *   *   *   *   *   *   *   *   *   *

August 22, 2011
Dear John,

Monica and I just got back from western Austria, and I was struck by how many churches, all Catholic, we saw. Literally every small town has its own church, and they are all unlocked through the day and are lovingly cared for. I was struck by the paintings of heaven on the ceilings of even the smallest of churches, and the fresh flowers that adorned the altars and the graves outside. You would have thought that Catholicism was flourishing in Austria as in no other place. Yet now only 66% say they are Catholic, as opposed to 89% several decades ago. And Sunday church attendance has fallen to 8% of those who claim to be Catholic. I really don't know what to make of this contrast between outer vigor and these lowly statistics.

Before getting down to what is really bothering me (you guessed it exactly), let me say a few words in Needleman's defense. In an earlier chapter he asks, "Who, looking at 'the starry sky above and the moral law within' can really maintain that all 'just happened'?" Later on he says that "God needs not just man, but awakened man, in order to act as God in the human world." And again: "The infinite universe exists as an immediate manifestation, creation, expression—the great Word—of that which is highest." I think it is clear that Needleman makes a distinction between God the Source and the universe, including ourselves, that He brings forth. He is no atheist. Nor is He a pantheist. But he is not a conventional theist either. Like me, he is sobered by the fact that our worthiest, most sincere prayers seldom or never get answered. What you call God's "pedagogical reserve"— a nice phrase—explains why God might not intervene when we think He should. The question for me, as for Needleman, is whether He ever does. And if He doesn't, then we must ask ourselves just how much of a person He is for us; for persons do intervene—at least good persons do—when they are asked to and think they can help.

I am not saying that God is not a Person, the supreme Person in fact, but only that He doesn't behave toward us in the manner we would expect Him to if He is a good person. So we are forced to imagine Him in a way that is new and at first rather off-putting. And that is what Needleman does so well. What he calls consciousness, or "my attention," is of the utmost preciousness for him—as it is for you and me. It "is seeded from some source higher than we know, a source searching for us even more than we are searching for it. I will call it, if I may, God." This is a God I can believe in. This God gives us "the energy that comes from above"—"a secret something within the body and soul of a human being." This isn't pantheism. Needleman consistently makes a distinction between the source of the energy and the energy itself. I think you should be pleased with this.

But let me confess that the sheer muscularity of our relation to God, as Needleman sees it, is at first scary. It is up to the individual human being to incarnate God's presence in the world—to "freely obey and be as God in the created world of his own body and thereby manifest toward man and nature what is needed from him." God is not going to help us from the outside. He has given us the means to help ourselves from within—the inner energy "that comes from above"—and hopes that we will be up to the task. Superficial begging for mercy, for help, for results is not going to get the job done. He is not a respecter of such prayer. So how should we pray? In any fashion that helps us identify with and act out of that divine gift, that grace, that energy "that comes from above" and helps us "be as God in the created world." And that means prayer deeper than words—prayer that flows out of our quiet depths. This is muscular religion, well beyond ordinary men and women, as Needleman admits.

So God is the Great Inviter, the Father who impregnates us with his energy and delights when some of us make good use of it. As for the others—and let me make it clear that I would not be at all surprised to find myself among this large lot!—there is plenty of time for their sanctification, probably not in this life, but in some afterlife venue or perhaps back on earth in a new body.

A final point. I do pray for those I love, mainly my children, but also my beloved deceased. Does God act from the outside to answer such prayers? I don't think so. But the energy He has imparted to us, if properly nurtured, will have an impact on those we pray for. God has given us the power to effect real results through our efforts at prayer, but He doesn't do it "from the outside." No wonder our prayers are so frequently "unanswered"! Again, appreciate the muscularity of religion looked at in this way. God is with us, ever so intimately with us, but He honors us by making us responsible for the results. Now that is an empowering relationship between persons! If He stepped in and solved our problems for us, we would be enfeebled as persons. I pause, stand back, and let myself meditate on the responsibility He has honored us with. And I am amazed!

I hope we are closer together than you at first thought.

Stafford

* * * * * * * * * * * *

August 27, 2011
Dear Stafford,

You may be right that Needleman is an honest-to-goodness theist. I was only giving you my impression of the passages you sent me. But some of the language you quote in your latest seems to me inconclusive, such as, "The infinite universe exists as an immediate manifestation, creation, expression—the great Word—of that which is highest." You can find many utterances just like this in Hegel, who is at bottom a pantheist. As I say, people who have come through Alcoholics Anonymous find ways of making their own the AA talk of a "higher power," and yet without returning to theism (some say the AA group is the higher power).

You ask for my reaction to your "muscular" take on God and religion. There is something to the idea of God empowering us rather than doing things for us—a kind of theological application of the saying that it is better to teach a hungry man how to fish than to give him a fish to eat. God doesn't let vaccines and airplanes fall from heaven, but lets us figure out how to make them. This idea of empowerment turns up in a certain way in the Catholic idea of justification as contrasted with the classical Lutheran idea: according to Trent we are really renewed from within when we are justified, and so are made able to perform good deeds, whereas Luther had said that in justifying us God just covers over our sin, like snow covers dung, leaving us unrenewed within and still unable to perform any good deeds of our own. But I have my reservations about your muscular religion.

1) I'm sure you know the line in the psalms, "Unless the Lord builds the house, they labor in vain who build it." I take this to mean that we can act fruitfully only by acting "in" God, by letting Him act through us, by making ourselves His instruments rather than acting entirely on our own. This is to me one of the primary religious experiences: the difference between acting out of God, in His name, through Him, with Him, and in Him, and acting on my own. The latter acting is in the end fruitless, barren, the former can bear unimagined fruit, as I have often experienced. What does this mean for our discussion? It means that our empowerment through God, which you want to acknowledge, is not an objective fact in the sense of being independent of our subjective awareness of it, but that it is subjective in the sense that our empowerment exists only by us acknowledging God, receiving His power, yielding to Him. This is a highly personal point of contact with God: we call upon Him, and He answers us, empowering us. I don't know if you accept this difference between objective and subjective. Do you think that our ability to act in a religiously fruitful way is like

our power of moving our limbs? that it is always at our disposal and does not have to be distinctly received in order to exist in us? Or do you think, as I do, that there is an interplay of God giving this ability and us receiving it? that people are very different with regard to the power of acting in a religiously fruitful way because they are very different in their openness to the grace of God?

2) I don't know how to find a place for the fallenness of man in your muscular scheme. Christianity sees all of us in the man beaten by robbers on the road to Jericho, lying wounded, unable to help ourselves, and sees Christ as the Good Samaritan who picks us up and binds our wounds. There seems to me to be a universal religious truth in this parable, and it is not clear that you can make any room for it in your muscular religion. You sound more like Nietzsche than like Christ. Mind you, I don't have to think of the God who forgives and redeems as "doing things" for me that I should learn to do for myself. The Christian idea is that I cannot redeem myself, and so God doesn't sit back and wait for me to do what I could never do. God doesn't expect us to work out our redemption in the way we work out the uses of fire or the growing of crops.

3) I detect a whiff of elitism in your muscular religion. Only a few heroic souls, capable of enduring a crushing weight of aloneness and responsibility, can really please God. Christianity seems to me more winning, more believable, more desirable, by the fact that it addresses the brokenhearted, the sick, the lame, the helpless, and does not pass them all by in favor the heavy-lifting spiritual athletes. But I repeat, His condescension to the weak and miserable does not involve doing for them what they should learn to do on their own; it involves doing for them what they could never do on their own.

4) I don't see why your idea of God empowering us to act has to exclude petitionary prayer. You are right to say that when a prayer seems to go unanswered we should ask whether God wants us to learn something that can only be learned by Him not answering our prayer. But you seem to be so taken by this new idea that you make it into the pattern of the relation between God and man, saying that God always wants us to learn to take care of all of our needs. If you think of the analogy with human parents, you find that sometimes wise parents do not intervene but let the child find his own way, but at other times they do intervene to help the child.

You like to work with such analogies, so why not think of God as a supremely wise parent?

5) I realize you will say that none of your prayers ever seem to be answered, and that therefore God's pedagogical reserve must be the all-controlling principle of His dealings with us. I understand what you mean by the appearance of prayers going unanswered, but I can't draw your conclusion because of all the scriptural admonitions to seek, to ask, to knock. There must be some hidden, less obvious answering of prayers, something that makes sense of the scriptural promises and of our experience of God's seeming silence. The empowerment I mentioned above in my first point constitutes a certain answer to prayer, and the forgiveness mentioned in 2 constitutes a further answer to prayer. But you are perhaps thinking of prayer that aims at some definite innerworldly event, like someone recovering from an illness. A positive answer to such a prayer is necessarily to some degree hidden under the web of secondary causes, if the recovery is not miraculous, for we can always wonder whether the person would have recovered anyway. But the circumstances surrounding the non-miraculous healing may be such that it is very plausible to see the hand of God in the healing, and in fact very difficult not to acknowledge it.

An example. I once heard Viktor Frankl tell about his perplexity regarding his opportunity to flee from Austria to the US in the late 1930's. The persecution of Jews was rising in Austria, but his parents were still in Vienna, and his invitation to the US was just for him and his wife. He went to St. Stephen's cathedral to pray for light. When he came home he found his father in despair over the razing of a Viennese synagogue by the Nazis. Out of piety his father had brought home a stone from the wreckage of the synagogue. Viktor Frankl examined the stone with him and they found on it the numeral IV; it was a fragment of the decalogue. Out of thousands of pieces of debris in the synagogue his father had picked up the number of the commandment to honor one's parents! He had picked it up just at the time when his son was praying. He who picked it up was the very person about whom his son was praying. Viktor Frankl immediately took this as the answer to his prayer: he declined his US option and he stayed with his parents in Vienna. Surely you are not going to tell me that Frankl acted superstitiously and that the more mature and "muscular" thing would have been to figure out by himself what he should do, without looking for any special divine help! The lives of believers are full of such answers to prayer. You will cut yourself off from the real faith of real believers if you try to discredit such petitionary prayer along the lines of your muscular religion.

If we are willing to live with such veiled forms of divine disclosure and divine intervention, we may in fact find many answers to our prayers. And then we can say that God's pedagogical reserve is not the only principle of His dealings with us.

6) You of all people should be open to such special helps, for you think that the dead are constantly sending us messages about the afterlife through mediums. They don't just let us figure out the afterlife on our own, but, on your view, they make special disclosures about it to us. If God allows this, why might not He make some special disclosures of His own in response to our prayers?

Enough discussion. Here is something deeper, taken from my own life. A few weeks ago I spent three days at the hermitage of a local Franciscan convent. No books of philosophy or theology; but prayer, and more than prayer, silence; reaching wordlessly upwards towards God, waiting to be reached by Him, abandoning myself into the mystery of God. No extraordinary experiences, no visions, nothing of the kind, but much peace. And you, my dear friend, were present to me.

In friendship,
John

* * * * * * * * * * *

September 18, 2011
Dear John,

I'll answer your last letter paragraph by paragraph, using your numbering.

1) You ask, "Do you think that our ability to act in a religiously fruitful way is like our power of moving our limbs? that it is always at our disposal and does not have to be distinctly received in order to exist in us?" I think

we get special help "from above" from time to time, but not necessarily because we ask for it, and not necessarily (or even usually) from God. There are many spiritual powers above us, and some of them, I suspect, know us and care for us by name. But I also think we have the power to help ourselves, and that this is probably the more usual means of acting in "religiously fruitful ways." And I suspect that God has made us the way we are in the expectation that we would try to work out our own problems without special help from Him. After all, God is present in our inner depths at all times. Thus we have the power to help ourselves at all times. This kind of help would be the norm.

2) I don't think of God as looking on at me as I go through life, so I don't think of Him as "sitting back and waiting" either. Does He really "jump in" at times when He sees I need special help, or when I ask with unusual sincerity—as if He were monitoring a video screen? This way of talking doesn't fit my experience. What does fit are those rare times when I've surrendered my life to Him not with the thought of some outcome, but with the confidence that whatever happened to me would be OK, that I would somehow get through my suffering. Those moments are important to me because I found great solace in them, and because in the end the situations did improve, whether by special help from above or by my own efforts I cannot say.

3) It is impossible for me to look around and not feel spiritually more advantaged than most of the world's population: I feel wondrously blessed. But at the same time I often wonder just how righteous I am in God's sight. I have made some serious mistakes in my life and a lot of minor ones, and it may well be that I overestimate my place in the scheme of things. I am also keenly aware that I am no "heavy-lifting spiritual athlete." My job constantly confronts me with those heavy lifters, and I am not in their league. As for the masses, or for that matter those materialist philosophers I work among, I do not have the same concern for them that you must have. They certainly won't be able to do, in this life, a lot of the things that you and I do, but someday they will—they'll have to, for God is not going to do it for them. God doesn't do the lifting for us, but there is infinite time at every soul's disposal to get around to doing it on their own. I know this sounds "muscular," but God is infinitely patient, and the gym never closes. Or so it seems to me.

4) Regarding petitionary prayer, on most mornings I pray in three ways—total time about twenty minutes, including distractions. I begin by asking God, the God within, the Holy Spirit if you like, to help me be a better person. I address God as Father, Mother, Light, Beloved, and Inner Heart. Then I call on whatever higher powers are interested in me and might be listening in. My routine is to ask for guidance and protection for my children, sometimes my parents, occasionally Lynette; this is true petitionary prayer. I end by trying to empty my mind of all content, with the help of a "prayer word," in the hope that I can have a more direct encounter with the Living God within. The Catholic writer Martin Laird is my guide in this difficult business. In his book *Into the Silent Land* he speaks of doorways that we pass through as we learn to contemplate. In the following passage he beautifully expresses how I think of God: "The doorways we begin to pass through are doorways into our own awareness, our own inner depths where we meet in this luminous darkness the gracious God who is already shining out of our own eyes, 'closer to me than I am to myself'." And what does God feel like for the contemplative? Laird writes: "There is a deeper core that is utterly free and vast and silent, that no thought or feeling has ever entered, yet every thought and feeling appears and disappears in it." Elsewhere he calls it a place in him "where no word has ever gone, but out of which the Word emerges."

5) So you see now that I am far from saying that our prayers are never answered. I believe they are, but in the way described above. My best guess is that Frankl's prayers were heard and answered, but probably not by God.

6) You wrote, "You of all people should be open to such special helps, for you think that the dead are constantly sending us messages about the afterlife through mediums. They don't just let us figure out the afterlife on our own, but, on your view, they make special disclosures about it to us." Yes, I place great importance on our ability to receive helpful, even saving messages from spirits. I think Frankl received such help. But then you write, "If God allows this, why might not He make some special disclosures of His own in response to our prayers?" He could, but he doesn't need to. He not only expects us to help ourselves, but to help each other. For that is the way we grow our souls, not only on physical planets like earth, but on astral (or spiritual) ones like those we'll enter at death. If God were to intervene and help us directly when we asked Him to, He would be depriving

spirits in higher places the opportunity to help those in lower. God is not so inefficient.

Are we closer than you thought?
Stafford

* * * * * * * * * * * *

October 17, 2011
Dear Stafford,

I just came across this passage in Ratzinger's book, *Truth and Tolerance*. It takes us back to the beginning of our exchange almost two years ago.

> It was Romano Guardini, above all, who indicated an important aspect of this basic pattern of Christian faith, which does not well up within us but comes to us from outside. Christianity, the Christian faith, he tells us, is not the product of our own experiences; rather, it is an event that comes to us from without. Faith is based on our meeting something (or someone) for which our capacity for experiencing things is inadequate. It is not our experience that is widened or deepened—that is the case in the strictly 'mystical' models; but something *happens*. The categories of 'encounter,' 'otherness' (*alterite*: Levinas), 'event,' describe the inner origins of the Christian faith and indicate the limitations of the concepts of 'experience.' ...This is exactly what is meant by the concept of revelation: something not ours, not to be found in what we have, comes to me and takes me out of myself, above myself, creates something new. That also determines the historical nature of Christianity, which is based on events and not on becoming aware of the depths of one's own inner self, what is called 'illumination.' The Trinity is not the object of our experience but is something that has to be uttered from outside, that comes to me from outside as 'revelation.' The same is true of the Incarnation of the Word, which is indeed an event and cannot be discovered in one's inner experience.

You may at first wonder why I am moved to share this passage with you, but I think you will recognize here the aspects of revelation I have stressed from the beginning. What I earlier called the gratuity of God's action in creating us and in redeeming us comes out in this passage in terms of "event" and "encounter." Very significant is the contrast Ratzinger draws between going in to one's innermost self and hearing a divine word spoken to us from without. The former can devolve into a monistic identification of self and God, and it is the latter that keeps alive a sense of God's otherness and of our creatureliness. Christian revelation involves both the former and the latter. The sense that our God is a "living" God is strongly conveyed when He acts like this from without, as when he sends His son as a human being. In my book on Newman's personalism I discuss pp. 214-217 an early sermon of Newman's in which he expresses the very idea about revelation that Ratzinger expresses here.

In friendship,
John

*   *   *   *   *   *   *   *   *   *   *

December 14, 2011
Dear John,

I look forward to your next message. Perhaps you are over eager to find differences where there are not any? Is there really just one way for Christians to think about God? That is not the impression I get from reading what the latest theologians are saying. I have in mind especially Marcus Borg and the mystic English Catholic Martin Laird. Perhaps we should at some point try to bridge our differences rather than exaggerate them. But I don't want to discourage you from teasing them out further if you think this is important. But perhaps you should say (again?) why this is important if you think it is. Would a Christian be endangering his relationship with God if he were to think as I do? Perhaps you should launch into a discussion of Jesus's place in the Trinity. The differences between us in that respect, however, are perhaps too obvious to mention.

Stafford

* * * * * * * * * * *

January 10, 2012
Dear Stafford,

I know that I seem to you to be fixated on our differences. My reason for focusing on them is simply that, ever since these differences emerged more than forty years ago, you have seemed to me to belittle them, to the point of saying that your theological position is rightly called a Christian one. I was recently reminded of one respect in which you, as it seems to me, have "fudged" on fundamental issues, namely your use of the Catholic sacraments. I found this in a letter I had written you in February, 2000:

> For years you have received the eucharist without believing what Catholics believe it to be. You know that a faithful priest would not be able to give you communion if he knew what you really believe and don't believe. You don't accept the Catholic terms for communion, but make up your own, bending the sacrament to your needs. You know that the priest's 'the body of Christ,' is a compact announcement of the faith of the Church, and that your 'amen' is meant to be an acceptance of this faith. You go through all these words without having this faith.

I don't know what your present practice is, and I don't bring this up as a busybody who is trying to police your actions; I bring it up as showing why you seem to me to be unwilling to let Catholic Christianity be itself and to acknowledge your own religious position as something else. The problem I see with your sacramental practice seems to me to repeat itself throughout your theoretical self-understanding. You seem to want the "prestige" of counting as a Christian even after you have moved far from Christian theism. This is what has provoked me to give primary attention to our differences. I think I wrote you earlier in our exchange that if we got our differences out in the open and acknowledged them, I would feel less inhibited about exploring all that we share-I would not feel that I was reinforcing a false assumption you were making.

I can show you what I mean by referring to your last full message to me in our exchange, your message of September 18. You make many good points in that message, and give me more insight into your idea of "intermediary beings" between us and God. But after all I did bring up this, which I don't think you responded to: "I don't know how to find a place for the fallenness of man in your muscular scheme. Christianity sees all of us in the man beaten by robbers on the road to Jericho, lying wounded, unable to help ourselves, and sees Christ as the Good Samaritan who picks us up and binds our wounds. There seems to me to be a universal religious truth in this parable, and it is not clear that you can make any room for it in your muscular religion. You sound more like Nietzsche than like Christ. Mind you, I don't have to think of the God who forgives and redeems as "doing things" for me that I should learn to do for myself. The Christian idea is that I cannot redeem myself, and so God doesn't sit back and wait for me to do what I could never do. God doesn't expect us to work out our redemption in the way we work out the uses of fire or the growing of crops."

In the Christian view we human beings are all involved in a primeval fall ("an aboriginal cataclysm," Newman says), a mysterious estrangement from God, a state in which sin and rebellion and death have gained power over us, so that we can be redeemed only by God breaking into human affairs and accomplishing for us what we could never accomplish for ourselves. You by contrast seem to envision a kind of self-salvation which God expects us to work out on our own. Just as we figure out how to treat illnesses with medications and surgery, and slowly advance from primitive medicine to scientific medicine, so we figure out how to live well, slowing advancing through many detours and mistakes to full spiritual maturity. Whether it's medicine or spiritual maturity, we do it on our own, according to your view, as I understand it. If I were to take a term from theology that I have used before in our correspondence, I would say that your "muscular" view of religion seems to me to end in a radically Pelagian religion. My point is not that your view is wrong, but just that it is not a Christian view. One can't replace God-who-redeems-man with man-who-redeems-himself, and still have the same religion.

What do you think, Stafford, is next for our exchange? Do you think we should continue on this line? Are there important things to be said here that we haven't said yet? Or strike out in some new direction? It is very rewarding to have this kind of close contact with you, and I think we should discern together its future direction.

In friendship,
John

* * * * * * * * * * *

February 1, 2012
Dear John,

Your last letter nicely sets the agenda for future exchanges.

You aptly summarize my view of religion—indeed of our place in the universe—in these words: "You by contrast seem to envision a kind of self-salvation which God expects us to work out on our own. Just as we figure out how to treat illnesses with medications and surgery, and slowly advance from primitive medicine to scientific medicine, so we figure out how to live well, slowing advancing through many detours and mistakes to full spiritual maturity." This is a fair description of my life, and I am deeply grateful for all the light that has gradually come my way, starting with my early boyhood in the Catholic Church, to which I was devoted. But to describe me as the spawn of Nietzsche is to go too far. You might as well describe me as the son of Lucifer! The truth is that I love God and pray to him daily, often fervently. But I dissociate myself from the following genocides, mass killings, and injustices committed, ordered, or approved by "God," as reported in the Old Testament:

24,000 Israelites who co-habited with Moabite women and worshipped Baal. "And the Lord said unto Moses, take all the heads of the people, and hang them up before the Lord against the sun."   Num. 25: 4,9

All the citizens of Jericho, except for a prostitute and her family. "And they utterly destroyed all in the city, man and woman, young and old, and oxen with the edge of the sword."   Josh. 6

50,700 people of Bethshemesh, struck dead by God, because a few of them who were working a field happened to glance into the Ark carrying the stone tablets of the "Ten Commandments" Judges 20:35

All the Amalekites killed by Saul upon God's orders. "Slay both man and woman, infant and suckling." I Sam. 15:3

Thou shalt not bow down thyself to them (graven images): for I the Lord thy God am a jealous God, visiting the iniquities of the fathers upon the children unto the third and fourth generation. Exodus 20:5

"Happy shall be he that taketh and dasheth thy little ones against the stones." Psalms 137:9. The "little ones" are the children of Babylon. The words—God's.

This list was collected by a friend of mine, and, as I say, I dissociate myself from these terrible deeds. God could not have done these things. The notion of Jesus's atoning death on the cross strikes me as a great step forward from these loathsome deeds, but as still somewhat primitive in its violence—and completely unnecessary.

But that is not to say that God never intervenes in the affairs of our planet—and here you might detect some movement in my theology. Lately I've been reading Plantinga—very much a personalist—and he has helped me see that God's occasional intervention in the world order should be no more unexpected than our own daily interventions. Nor are these divine interventions any more "miraculous" than our own. Persons with power do intervene. It is natural for them to do so. But please don't take this to mean that I am walking away from my muscular form of religion: God might be the "Good Samaritan who picks us up and binds our wounds," but He doesn't prevent the wounds from occurring in the first place. Nor does he pick us up without our participation.

You go on to say, "My point is not that your view is wrong, but just that it is not a Christian view. One can't replace God-who-redeems-man with man-who-redeems-himself, and still have the same religion." As you know, there are many Christians, including some of its best minds, who would disagree with you. They don't derive their identity from the Church's councils, but from the example and the preachings of Jesus as found in the synoptic gospels. Marcus Borg is one of their leaders, and he is typical of the liberal wing of Christianity. Just as Jesus was a reformist Jew condemned by the entrenched authorities for breaking Sabbath restrictions and other rules of the religion, so Borg and other reform-minded Christians are reproached for their views by traditionalists like yourself. "They are not Christians," say their detractors, but are pretenders unjustly enjoying the "prestige" of counting as a Christian. Borg could have left Christianity and joined some New Age community, but his love for the Church, his spiritual home, drove him to try to change it instead. When I wrote for *NCR*, that was my intention as well. I love its rituals, its (Anglican) hymnology, its high moral idealism, and, above all, its personal Godhead. I recognize, as I hope you do, that we, as children, would have been devout worshippers of Krishna if we had been born into certain Hindu families. But we weren't, so Hinduism will not serve as our spiritual home, even though the intense incarnational personalism is as present in most expressions of Hinduism as in Christianity.

People like Borg are not trying to destroy Christianity from the inside, but save it for future generations for whom atonement theology seems like a lookback to ancient Jewish themes, one that doesn't seem plausible for many God-loving individuals. One of the strongest spiritual communities in Bakersfield calls itself the Center for Spiritual Living. This is a God-centered New Age community composed mostly of former Christians. I've thought of joining it, for its theology is in many respects closer to mine than Christianity's. But it tends to put too happy a face on human nature and human destiny. So I'll continue to attend the local downtown Anglican church, with its beautiful setting, music, and rituals; its thoughtful, well-prepared, often challenging sermons; and its several living saints.

I agree with you that we humans are estranged from God. All religions I've studied with the exception of Buddhism agree, too. But Christianity is the only one to require an atoning sacrifice before God will forgive us our sins. I wish I could convey to you how strange this notion seems to me now—not so much wrong, but strange. God is well aware of our predicament. He wants to see what we will do without being coerced. Those of us who choose wisely will be rewarded, and those who don't won't—though there will be other chances for them to use their freedom more wisely. Where is the need for a sacrifice? On the other hand, atonement theology has immense power for those who can believe in it. That God would die for us requires a love that is unfathomable, and the heart of the believer can only swell with gratitude and adoration at the thought of it. This I grant. The problem is that for most people not brought up in the faith, and to almost all outsiders, this kind of thinking doesn't make sense. Ask any Jew or Muslim. I'd like to see Christianity remove such stumbling blocks.

As for receiving communion at a Catholic church, I have dithered over this for many years. I don't like saying yes to things I don't believe, but I also believe that Jesus intended his words to be understood metaphorically. The bread and the wine were to be understood, I believe, as symbols of his continuing presence among his closest disciples after his death. I respect the Catholic view that its priests can literally turn the elements into the body and blood of Christ. Hinduism's priests are given similar powers when they consecrate images of Krishna or Shiva, and the images become the actual seats of divine presence. I respect all these beliefs and see their power for many people, but I do not share them. Does this mean I should stay away from the sacrament since I don't share these ideas? It's not clear to me why I should as long as I am not an occasion of sin for potential human judges occupying the pews around me. I suspect most pastors would rather have my capital than my orthodoxy if forced to choose. Of course, if my receiving the sacrament had the power of offending God, that would be a different matter. But I can only imagine God saying, "Are you kidding?"

I think the main thing that has separated us in these matters, John, is my in-depth study of other religions. They all seem obviously manmade. So when you ask me to consider how I can take communion given my beliefs, I look past all these manmade ordinances and rules and trust my own reading. Religion, after all, is an intensely private affair, and rules that are well-intended cannot possibly cover all the varieties of human beings that come through the door. The Catholic Church should be quick to offer guidance, but slow to set requirements and pronounce anathemas. So I end by disagreeing with you when you say, "One can't replace God-who-redeems-man with man-who-redeems-himself, and still have the same religion." What makes a man a Christian is his love of Jesus' teachings and example, as seen in the Gospels. Anyone who tries to follow Christ is on the road to salvation and deserves to be called a Christian. And that would include Catholics, Protestants, Greek and Russian Orthodox, Mormons, Pelagians, and (God help us!) Jehovah's Witnesses.

You might think this permissive approach would lead to chaos, but it hasn't in Hinduism, the most permissive of all religions, with no central pope or governing body. I favor their inclusive approach.

Stafford

*　　*　　*　　*　　*　　*　　*　　*　　*　　*　　*

February 9, 2012
Dear Stafford,

Many thanks for your last message, and for your patience with my slow pace. Let me qualify my association of you with Nietzsche. There is in Nietzsche a certain esteem for strength and a corresponding scorn for weakness of the broken-hearted. I thought I caught a whiff of this ranking when I read what you said about muscular religion. I don't mean that you are given over to the will-to-power, or that you are eagerly proclaiming the death of God, or that you think with Nietzsche that the Christian concern for the weak is a sign of *ressentiment* directed against the strong. I know that you and I would stand together against Nietzsche on many important issues.

The question of receiving Catholic communion without having Catholic belief about the sacrament doesn't seem so complex to me; there seems to me an obvious issue of integrity. In saying "the body of Christ" the Catholic priest means to announce the "real presence." It doesn't matter whether you think that Christ meant the talk of his body and blood only metaphorically; the priest who speaks to you in communion means it literally, and your "amen" must be meant literally in order to be truthful. As I see it, you get communion only because you deceive the priest; if he knew that you don't believe what Catholics believe about the body and blood of the Lord, he would not be at liberty to give you communion. You often hear at masses with many non-Catholics in attendance an announcement about the sacrament being only for the Catholics. The Church means to reserve the sacrament for those of the "household of faith." Is this not an intention to be respected? You get the sacrament by misrepresenting yourself—isn't that enough to settle the matter ethically? Episcopal churches are of course another matter, since they do not link receiving the sacrament with sharing a particular faith.

By the way, it is not so easy to say that Christ spoke only metaphorically in speaking of giving his body and blood. Why did many who had been following him, take offense at this teaching? Why was it a scandalous, divisive teaching (John 6)? Why didn't Jesus stop the disciples who were going away, by saying, "You misunderstand me, my friends, I'm only proposing a symbolic ritual of remembrance"?

I grant you that the Old Testament passages that you bring up contain some great difficulties for Christians. I recently heard a panel of theologians trying to make sense of these passages, and none of them satisfied me. I agree with you that we can't think that the God of Jesus Christ really authorized the slaughter of all men, women and children in Jericho and other towns. And yet at the same time Christians believe that the Jews really are a chosen people, and indeed that they are constituted as a people by Jahweh's preferential love for them. There must be a way of affirming their special relation to Jahweh without thinking of the slaughters as directly commanded by God. I find helpful the way von Hildebrand expresses this special relation in a paper entitled "The Jews and the Christian West," from 1937. He writes: "Israel was the only people to whom, before the fullness of time, God showed his countenance, the only people he called by name, in such a way that they came into full consciousness of the need for redemption and cried out to heaven for two thousand years: 'Show us your face Lord and we will be saved.' Objectively, the entire world at that time stood in a state of advent, but Israel alone was aware of this." God awakened in the Jews a longing for a redeemer, and fulfilled this longing in Jesus. I realize that you don't believe this, but my point right now is that this expresses a chosen-ness that has no intrinsic tie to the stories of slaughter.

I know that you will say that the history of the Jews is all-too-human, and that every appearance of chosenness can be explained away by natural causes and by merely human dynamics. But the Catholic imagination can envision divine election at work in the midst of all manner of human conditioning. Just as there is a divine spark in man, working itself out in evolutionary development but not deriving from it, so with the Jews and the Christian Church. Just as you can, if you choose, see only natural causes at work in the emergence of man, and deny the divine spark in him that "comes from without" (as already Aristotle put it), so you can, if you choose, see only natural causes and historical conditioning at work in Jewish history. This analogy between God's image in man, which serves to set man above all other creatures, and His presence in the Jewish people and the Christian church, which serves to set Christianity above all other religions, has already come up in our exchange. The root issue here, as I see it, is not exactly Jewish election, but the way of conceiving God's activity in the finite world and in human affairs.

As for the sacrificial and atoning death of Jesus, there is one aspect of it that seems to me to have a deep religious appeal, an appeal that you are sure to feel: God descends into the depths of the human condition, undergoing abandonment and rejection and enduring human brutality and injustice. When people point to the evil that is rampant in the world and ask why God does not stop it, Christians can say that, however one explains it, it is not an evil that God sees at a distance, but an evil that He has personally "tasted." He has achieved solidarity with all sufferers, becoming one of them. He does not ask us to suffer while He remains unscathed, but has willed to suffer with us. I don't know how any non-Christian religion could offer a comparable comfort to those who mourn and grieve. Looked at this way, the crucifixion is not the residue of brutal religious practices, but it is God's way of entering into solidarity with those who suffer brutality. In this respect it is not strange—it is full of divine extravagance, but not strange, and it makes a certain sense. You ask why the death of the God-man would be necessary. Necessary for what? It may be very necessary for God to achieve the solidarity with us human beings that He wants to have.

Who counts as a Christian is in part a verbal dispute and is resolved by agreeing on a definition of Christian. If anyone who admires Jesus Christ, and draws inspiration from some of his deeds and teachings, is a Christian, then most Moslems are Christians, many atheists are Christians, and you too are a Christian. I have of course been taking Christian in a narrower sense in asking whether your theology is Christian. This is more or less the same sense of Christian that is at stake when people call

Christianity a world-religion and distinguish it from Islam, Hinduism, etc. To be aligned with Christianity as a world-religion, takes more than respect for some moral teachings of Jesus, doesn't it?

But when we turn our attention from "Christianity" to "Catholicism" we can no longer ignore the ecclesial dimension; to speak of a cutting-edge Catholic who loves Jesus but rejects the Nicene Creed, doesn't make much sense.

Which of these different strands of discussion will be most fruitful to pursue? I greet you with great affection and deep respect.

John

* * * * * * * * * * * *

February 26, 2012
Dear John,

Our debate has been over a Christian understanding of God. A primary commitment that we share is God as Person. God is the Supreme Person. We've been trying to work out what this means and what the implications of it are. Among other things, it could mean—and does mean for a person of faith— that God and humans can have a relationship since we, too, are persons. Thus prayer makes sense.

And if we can have a relationship, then it follows that God understands something of our plight; otherwise we would be talking "past each other," as they say. Now if God understands something of our plight, it stands to reason that God must experience suffering Himself (Herself) in some manner or other. The next step I cannot take with you, but I do not deny that it has great appeal: that is, that God descended into flesh and experienced physical suffering to show us how much He really does understand our plight. This is a divine motivation that I would be delighted to find at the foot of the cross. The reason I reject it is that there is too great a difference between the way I think of God and the way I think of man. As John Hick put it, man is a creature, and God is a non-creature, so they cannot be one and the same being—as every Muslim, incidentally, would see as self-evident. Still, it is a lovely idea for the pious. What is not so lovely is the doctrine of atonement. That God should have so unrealistic a view of human beings that He cannot be reconciled with them unless He Himself die a violent death for them on the cross is exceedingly strange. Therein is a motivation utterly different from the earlier one. What starts out as an all-too-human policy of exclusion—"You aren't good enough to be in my presence, foul sinner, unless you pay an impossibly high price"—is stood on its head by God's paying the price for us. How very odd! Why adopt the over-the-top policy of exclusion in the first place? Why not save Himself the trouble of intervening so heroically, and at such great cost, on our behalf? God did not have to do any of this.

Men sometimes behave this way, however, and we usually see through their motivation. Someone does you a great wrong, and instead of prosecuting him, you not only forgive him but go out of your way to do something extremely nice for him in the hope of winning him over, or at least of embarrassing him. It almost never works. It doesn't work because in the right order of things the offender should do something nice for his victim. The research I've done on the afterlife reveals exactly this law of nature. It is this law that is behind the wonderfully sane Catholic belief in purgatory. While in purgatory it is up to us to pay the price of our salvation by reforming ourselves. That is all that ever should have been required. Substitutionary atonement not only presupposes a God who has little comprehension of human weakness, but subverts the natural order.

So let us have a God who suffers with us, but for no other motivation than to understand and love us better.

This unGodly trait of exclusivity also turns up in the Catholic insistence on a particular understanding of what happens at Communion. There will always be literalists, but for the Church to validate only the literal interpretation of the priest's words—and to exclude any other possible understanding—is unpastoral. It turns away people who love their God, love Jesus' gospel, and love the ritual of the Mass, but who cannot accept the scandalous teaching (as they see it) of transubstantiation—which they view as magical. That the Church should forbid these people from accepting the sacrament is a great mistake. These days most well educated young people are not capable of believing something their senses tell them isn't so. My only reason for avoiding Communion in a Catholic Church is to not give offense to fellow congregants. That God might care one way or the other strikes me as infinitely unlikely.

You write, "If anyone who admires Jesus Christ, and draws inspiration from some of his deeds and teachings, is a Christian, then most Moslems are Christians, many atheists are Christians, and you too are a Christian." Of course, it takes that and much more to be a Christian. Above all, it takes a desire to worship with other Christians while recognizing the authority of the two Great Commandments—which would exclude all atheists and many Muslims. As for the Nicene Creed, it was the product, let us not forget, of the Emperor Constantine's demand that the assembled bishops formulate a creed that spelled out once and for all who Christ was and, even more, who God was—thus the Trinity. Constantine's motive was primarily political: he wanted to stop the wrangling among Christians and bring about unity among them. The bishops, of course, believed that the Holy Spirit guided them to a truth that they could not have come to on their own. But today large numbers of Christians worshipping in churches of all denominations quietly disbelieve that Jesus was conceived by the Holy Spirit and was born of a virgin. As for the Trinity, was it wise for mere men to assume such Godlike authority? The Nicene Creed and its simpler cousin the Apostle's Creed become more and more difficult to accept at face value with every passing generation, as so many of our children are making clear. I deeply regret that Christianity is stuck with Nicaea. A little later I'll share with you what I wish the bishops had declared.

Stafford

* * * * * * * * * * * *

March 6, 2012
Dear Stafford,

I must say with sadness that your last message made me feel more keenly than ever before the gulf between us.

First let me correct a point about the Catholic understanding of the redemption. It is the common opinion among Catholic theologians that God could have ended the estrangement between Himself and us human beings by a simple decree; the Incarnation and the Paschal Mystery were not the only possible instruments for accomplishing our redemption. He chose these instruments, they say, in order to express certain things: not only the enormity of sin, but also the unimaginable reach of His love.

On the latter subject I just came across this in von Balthasar, who is referring to Romans 8:32 ("He who did not spare His own Son but handed him over for us all, how will He not also give us everything else along with him?"): "...the Son's obedient willingness to enter death for the sake of everyone is united with the Father's willingness to sacrifice to the point of not holding back His Son in order to give us everything. In this, God is not only with us, as in the Old Testament's 'Emmanuel,' but is ultimately 'for us,' His chosen ones. In this He has not merely given us something great, but has given us everything He is and has. Now God is so completely on our side that any indictment against us loses all its force."

If I understand von Balthasar rightly, his thought can be clarified by referring to a well-known difference among human beings: some act to confer benefits on others, but in such a way as to withhold themselves, the benefits perhaps even functioning as a substitute for real self-giving, whereas others confer benefits in such a way as really to give themselves, really to make themselves radically available. It is as if redemption by simple decree of God would have made God like the first kind of benefactor, whereas the way He has in fact chosen in Christ makes him more like the second kind of benefactor. This is why I said in my last message that there is in Christianity an incomparable solidarity of God with us, an incomparable way of him being for us. This takes us far deeper into the Paschal Mystery than any juridical theology of atonement and "satisfaction." I bring this up because it seems to be a way of thinking about the crucifixion and resurrection in terms that are sure to connect with your own strongest religious concerns.

Let me now try to get to one of the main roots of our disagreements over what is Christian and what is not. It seems to me that Catholicism forms a certain whole, and that you do not do justice to this whole. You want Catholicism to develop in the direction of your own religious views, and are exasperated when it doesn't, and you don't see, as it seems to me, the kind of incoherence that would result from blending certain of your views with Catholic views. Here are some examples taken from your last message. You say that the Nicene Creed was good for the 4th century but no longer for us, implying thereby that Catholicism will be enhanced by adopting a relativism of dogma, as if what Newman calls the "dogmatical principle" were not constitutive of Catholicism. In cancelling that creed you would also give up the faith in the divinity of Christ, as if that were, from the point of view of Catholic identity, a negotiable article of faith. You think the entire sacramental system (and not just the Eucharist) should go, so as to make Catholicism more acceptable to educated young people who only trust their senses. My point is not that you should believe these Catholic things, but that you should acknowledge how they hang together and form a coherent whole, and are constitutive of Catholicism. You should at least acknowledge that if we were to abandon even some of these things, we would not update Catholicism and pare away inessential accretions, but would abolish Catholicism in favor of another religion. You call this "ungodly exclusivity," but Catholics say we are just abiding by the principle of identity as formulated by Bishop Butler: "Each thing is itself and is not another."

The contemporary world is full of incoherence of the kind I am talking about. People want sex apart from parental responsibility, as if sexual intimacy suffered no loss by being sterilized. They want marital union apart from the complementarity of man and woman, and very soon they will not know why marital union should be restricted to two persons. They seem to think that the whole world of man and woman is subject to the "cut and paste" function on their computers; they can clip this and paste that, without giving a thought to whether there are deep essential structures of creation that resist such cut and paste operations, such that certain things dissolve into incoherence when separated from some essential complement. Just the other day I was listening online to a smart-aleck young atheist who thinks that there is no problem in having all the consolation that religion provides without having any religious belief. He clips out "consolation" from religion and he wants to paste it in to "atheism." It never seems to occur to him that the world has to be in a certain way if consolation is going to be meaningfully motivated and be worthy of a rational being. Now I know well that your religious position has vastly more depth than that of this atheist who wants to keep some elements of religion. But at the same time I must say that you seem to me to want to clip a few fragments out of your ancestral Catholicism, like purgatory and the example of Jesus, and then paste them into the theism of John Hick, and to present the result as

Catholicism the way it should be. I want to say to you that the result is religious incoherence. You would show far more respect for Catholicism if you would let it be itself and you be yourself, instead of insisting that it be more like you.

Here I think we come to the root of our disagreement over the respect that non-believers owe to the sacramental body of the Lord. For a long time I couldn't understand why you would want to put yourself into the role of an unwanted intruder, which is what you do when you receive Communion without believing. I couldn't understand why this point, when I raised it with you, made no impression on you. Then it came to me that the reason you don't respect the way the Catholic church reserves the sacrament for believing Catholics is that you think the Church is doing something wrong by reserving the sacrament in this way, and that the Church really ought to open the sacrament to anyone who wants it, regardless of their eucharistic and christological views. So your practice in church is, I suppose, felt by you to be the vanguard of a change that ought to be made, and will surely come in time. But I object to this stance of yours on grounds of general coherence: Catholicism does not become more itself by abandoning its eucharistic faith and practice, it rather thereby admits a foreign body into itself and tends to come apart. If you could find a way to let Catholicism be itself while you remain yourself, you would stop trying to recast the sacrament in your image, and you wouldn't take such liberties with the sacrament. My "unwelcome intruder" argument would say more to you.

As I write this, Stafford, I feel by anticipation the intense resistance you will have to all that I am saying. I suspect that we have reached the point of understanding each other that Newman has in mind when he says, "When men understand each other's meaning, they see, for the most part, that controversy is either superfluous or hopeless." Not that we can't continue to exchange ideas on all that is of concern to us, but this particular thread of discussion extending over almost two years (concerning what is and what is not Christian) has perhaps reached its natural end. I know you will challenge me if you think I am calling this prematurely. I have no desire to break off unilaterally.

In friendship,
John

* * * * * * * * * * *

March 15, 2012
Dear John,

Let me start by responding to your last point. I don't become exasperated when I see Catholicism resisting change. I'm in no position to change it, and the most I can feel is regret that it remains intransigent on certain points. That it insists on Jesus being God is understandable. The world has always turned on exaggerations. Men from all cultures have been divinizing their hero-saints down through the ages. One has only to recall the thesis and many examples of this in Joseph Campbell's *Hero with a Thousand Faces.* One thing that troubles me about this tendency, however, is what it does to outsiders who can't share these forms of concretized faith. They are excluded and sometimes persecuted. But even more troubling is that these various forms are not truly, in my view, what their enthusiasts claim for them. It simply isn't possible for me as an adult to believe about Jesus what I found so easy to believe as a child. God, a universe designed by Him, his love for his creatures, a meaningful and joyous afterlife if deserved, accountability, spirit helpers, prayer, the moral law written in our hearts, hero saints to look up to and emulate—these are the things I hold sacred today. These add up to more than "a few fragments." Are you not forgetting this impressive ledger of beliefs we share, and that I share with Christians, especially Catholic Christians, when you react with sadness to the things that divide us? Like you, I yearn to develop myself in a saintly direction. The challenge for both of us, I imagine, is very similar. Our central struggle is the same: transforming ourselves into more worthy, God-pleasing beings. Do we need to share the same dogma to relate to each other's struggle and accomplishment? And do you really want to exclude me from the Christian family because I don't equate Jesus with God or see Jesus literally in the Eucharist or because I believe in rebirth for many of us?

You write, "Catholicism does not become more itself by abandoning its eucharistic faith and practice, it rather thereby admits a foreign body into itself and tends to come apart." However: Did Catholicism not unravel a little when it explicitly endorsed salvation for non-Christians who follow their religion in earnest at the Second Vatican Council? I think it did, and that it needed to. And 500 years ago it condemned Protestants. The Church has changed and will continue to change. Is it admitting a foreign body by ordaining married converts from Anglicanism to the priesthood? Or when it ordains women later this century? Or permits married gays to receive the Eucharist without fear of sinning? I don't think so. And if in the next century it redefined God in a manner that included Motherliness as well as Fatherliness, would that be a foreign body? Or if it allowed Catholics to believe in reincarnation without fear of sin? What you are calling coherence, I am suggesting, is not derived from something essential, but from doctrines laid down by fallible theologians down through the centuries. What you call coherence comes from what you are comfortable believing, not some sort of irresistible internal logic. I believe this will become clearer to you once you've been dead for a few years and see the better possibilities afforded by the luminous world ahead of us. One thing will become frighteningly clear to both of us then: the degree to which we didn't measure up to what we set out to achieve, and the superior attainments of many who did not share our personalist philosophy, including many Buddhists and even an occasional atheist.

We return to an old subject when you question my decision to receive the Eucharist at Mass. In the past I have stayed away from the sacrament, though not every time, when I knew you were in church and would notice. And I'll continue to follow that practice when you are present. I don't want to be offensive. But when you are not present, I will continue to approach the altar. As I see it, receiving communion is part of the ritual, like reciting the creed, or saying the prayers of the faithful. At baptisms do I really mean what I say when I agree to do all in my power to support the newly baptized infant in her Christian life? Of course not. But I say the words anyway. They show support for the parents of the infant and stimulate reverent emotions. And Jesus himself constantly used sacred hyperbole: "If your eye be an occasion of sin, tear it out . . ." And I don't think he had anything like transubstantiation in mind when he told his disciples, "This is my body . . . my blood." So when I say "Amen," it is for me a way of saying, "I remember you." Of course I have no quarrel with people who believe in the Real Presence. Their belief only increases their piety and is for them a blessing.

Finally, regarding the quotations by von Balthasar, let me say that I have never found inspiration in Abraham's willingness to sacrifice his son Isaac. I find the thought frankly horrifying and wish it were not read to the faithful from the pulpit. So you can't expect me to endorse the Heavenly Father's willingness to sacrifice his Son in a similar act. That God suffers with us in some deeply mysterious way is more than enough and is more than we deserve. I ask no more. I do, however, recognize the power of the Cross when seen as a metaphor for God's suffering. It sets Christianity apart from every other theistic religion and rightly emphasizes the suffering that sin carries in its wake. Our world needs such a reminder. But when Christians turn the metaphor into a juridical transaction, weighing our sin against Christ's atonement, the beautiful metaphor is besmirched. And when they go further and insist that men and women sign on to the deal before the transaction can work on their behalf, they scandalize all who cannot sign on.

Stafford

* * * * * * * * * * * *

June 20, 2012
Dear Stafford,

I'm back. Many thanks for the beautiful images of the cathedral (the new one in Barcelona?) How good it would be if we could experience it together, like we did those wonderful French cathedrals many years ago.

I don't know if you had a chance to read the Sokolowski chapter on the Christian understanding of creation out of nothing. As I say, it articulates well some things that I have wanted to say from the beginning of our exchange. Here are a few representative sentences.

> According to the natural and spontaneous understanding, the divine and the nondivine form parts of a larger whole. The divine may be recognized as the exemplary, the controlling, the encompassing, the best, and even in some sense the origin, but it is not normally conceived as that which could be, in undiminished goodness and excellence, even if everything else were not. … For the pagan the whole is essentially prior to both the divine and the rest of being, but for the Christian the divine could

be the whole, even if it is not, since it is meaningful to say, in Christian belief, that God could be all that there is.

Of particular importance for our exchange is this: "For the Incarnation to be possible, the divine nature must not be conceived as one of the natures within the whole of the world." He explains:

> In the natural order of things, a union such as that of the Incarnation is impossible, and to assert such a union would be to state an incoherence... In the natural order of things, each being is one kind of being. In being what it is, each thing excludes other kinds of being. A human person is not and cannot be a tree; a lion is not and cannot be a diamond. And since the divine [conceived] as part of the world is one of the natures in the world, [it follows that] in the natural order of things a god, as understood by pagan thinking, cannot be human. A god could become human only by becoming less than a god, or not fully human, or by being only apparently human or only apparently divine, or by becoming some new kind of thing different from both the divine and the human.

I am not arguing that you should believe these things, only that you should acknowledge that Christians who do believe them hold a distinctive position, not to be run together with other religious positions. You seem to me to commit this mistake of running together when, in your last message, you throw the Christian understanding of the incarnation in with all the tales about gods collected by Joseph Campbell.

Perhaps the Sokolowski insights enable us to revisit the issue, raised in my last message and picked up in your last message back to me, the issue of the inner coherence of the different "elements" of Christian belief. I find that he brings to light a strong internal connection of Christian creation and the Incarnation. He says that the latter is incoherent without the former, for the reasons just mentioned. In another place he says that the Christian understanding of God's providence, a providence usually exercised without any miraculous disruptions of the natural order of things, is based on the divine transcendence that is implied by Christian creation. Indeed, his idea that the Christian way of distinguishing God and the world is a "dimensional" distinction means precisely that it draws most of the other Christian beliefs into a new dimension, so that these are not just added to Christian creation but are situated by it in a new frame of reference. Thus you can't drop the Christian understanding of creation and retain intact the Christian belief in the incarnation, in the eucharist, in providence.

Around the time of the Vatican Council I once heard a homily in which the preacher affirmed that there literally is no afterlife, that Christianity is exclusively about this life, that death ends everything. About the same time a book appeared with the title, *The Gospel of Christian Atheism*. You probably feel as I felt: these are not possible Christian positions. Thus I can't imagine that you would want to deny the existence of "internal coherences" and "internal incompatabilities" among religious beliefs, or would want to psychologize these away as being nothing but a matter of what we are accustomed to, or would think that religious beliefs can be "cut" and "pasted" like we cut and paste text on our computers. Even though we often make mistakes about what coheres and what does not cohere, this only serves to admonish us to caution in making coherence claims, it does not serve to show that we should not even look for coherences among religious beliefs.

And so when I said in my last message that the Incarnation is constitutive for Catholic Christianity, I wasn't saying anything so very controversial. When I said that that particular prolongation of the Incarnation which Catholics venerate as the eucharistic presence is also constitutive for Catholic Christianity, that too need not be controversial between you and me. You mention scriptural hyperbole; but just as you don't think that the affirmation of life-after-death is hyperbolic talk, not to be taken literally, so neither do Catholics think the words of Jesus about his body and blood (both in the eucharistic discourse in John and in the last supper accounts in the synoptics) can be taken hyperbolically. And just as you do not think it is a small matter to switch from literal to hyperbolic talk about the afterlife, so we do not think it is a small matter to make this switch with respect to the incarnation and the eucharist.

You mention the shift at Vatican II with regard to non-Christians. But I don't think you state it quite right; stated correctly it is easy to recognize as a legitimate development of Catholic belief and not the intrusion of a foreign element. As I understand it, the Council taught that non-Christians who follow their conscience can participate in the paschal mystery in some way known only to God. This means that they too can be saved through the death and resurrection of Christ, even though they do not know Christ and so do not have faith in Him. But they are not saved through their non-Christian religion but through Christ.

I am still puzzled that you would recite the creed without believing it, and say what believers say at baptisms and at holy communion, but again without believing it. It seems to me a cheapening of religious language. Words are evacuated of their meaning—all for the sake of a little fellowship. I think you would show believers more respect by abstaining from using the language that they use to express their faith and that they mean quite literally. By your present practice you seem to be saying, "All these religious professions don't mean anything anyway, or if they mean something, it doesn't much matter what they mean; the only important thing is that we are all together in a liturgical celebration." It is this stance of yours that makes me feel much more divided from you than your heterodox views do.

In friendship,
John

*　*　*　*　*　*　*　*　*　*　*　*

June 28, 2012
Dear John,

I read Sokolowski's article with interest. Thank you. But it seems to me that anyone who is serious about Christian theism would have to *deny*, not affirm, that God could ever have been "the whole"—all there is. If God were the whole, there would be nothing outside Himself to pour his love into. You could claim that God's need to love would be satisfied by the three Persons' love for each other—making creation unnecessary—but that kind of love strikes me as narcissistic. A full-bodied, robust love—agape—is always directed to the other: to benefiting that other, giving some good to that other that it didn't already have. How could there ever have been a time in all eternity when there was nothing to direct this robust type of love to? Father, Son, and Holy Spirit lack nothing, so they could not have been the recipients of this kind of love. Therefore a universe—an Other—must always have existed. That is not to say, however, that God's stature and uniqueness are somehow diminished by a coeternal universe. Nothing outside Himself compelled Him to create it. It was his own innate nature—and only that—that gave rise to the universes that He has lovingly created throughout endless time.

We agree that Christianity makes no sense if there is no afterlife—no need to discuss this. And I grant that if anything as strange as God becoming man can happen, then a piece of bread turning into God is not that much stranger. So I see your point about internal coherence. But when you take scriptural testimony as evidence for both these events, as if that settles the issue, then I must demur. Further, I don't find it helpful to compare such evidence with the enormously impressive evidence for an afterlife reaching us from many sources, both traditional and recent. My confidence in the reality of an afterlife approaches certainty. One of the reasons for this confidence has been argued convincingly both by Newman and yourself. I have in mind the utter incompatibility between physical things and the phenomenology of consciousness, and thus their radical difference and destiny.

I've been reading Newman lately from the little book you gave Louie ten years ago. I mention this to try and dissuade you from the claim that "non-Christians are not saved through their non-Christian religion but through Christ." Newman writes: ". . the church of God ever has had, and the rest of mankind never have had, authoritative documents of truth, and appointed channels of communication with Him. The word and the sacraments are the characteristic of the elect people of God; but all men have had more or less the guidance of Tradition, in addition to those internal notions of right and wrong which the Spirit has put into the heart of each individual."

It seems to me that Newman grants more power to non-Christian religion than you do. And that, in my view, is to his credit. He strikes me as quite progressive for his time.

Let me try again to help you understand what it's like to be me when confronted with Sunday morning Mass, especially the Creed. You might remember the reading from Job this past Sunday. God said to Job: "Who shut up the sea behind doors when it burst forth from the womb, when I made the clouds its garment and wrapped it in thick darkness, when I fixed limits for it and set its doors and bars in place, when I said, 'This far you may come and no farther; here is where your proud waves halt.'" No one believes this really happened; we see here the primitive worldview of a pre-scientific age. Yet the passage gets read anyway, for it links us to our spiritual past. In the same spirit I say the Nicene Creed. Now I will grant you I'd much prefer that the Creed not be said in the service. I don't like saying things I don't mean; it doesn't feel good. I have to work at remembering what I'm doing. But the Eucharist is another thing. I don't think Jesus intended to be taken literally when he said, "This is my body." It seems to me much more reasonable to think he wanted his disciples to think of him as spiritually present with them when they broke bread following his death. It's common, after all, for people to speak of the dead in this way. So for me the Eucharist is a gathering of present-day disciples at a common table to remember and celebrate his life, just as Jesus intended.

Now let me get to the gist of our disagreement over the nature of God. The more I've thought about who God is, the more comfortable I've gotten with the philosophy known as Vedanta, as I said earlier. By this I mean, as I've explained before in somewhat different words, that the soul is a tiny cell in the Divine Substance, not a creation of something that had no substance at all before it was created (*creatio ex nihilo*).

Now why would I choose Vedanta over Christianity on this subject? Mainly because of what seems to happen during prayer. If I pray to God as Other, I am asking Him to do things for me and those I love—to intervene. As I've shown earlier, I believe there are serious problems with this interventionist view. Too often God does not intervene in situations where the best of us would intervene every time. You don't have to search beyond your own family for examples. And this leads to the conclusion that God is not present, not nearby, not concerned, not even aware. But if my very soul-substance and God are one, if I am that tiny God-cell mentioned above, then I can never doubt God's presence. I will always know that, whatever happens to me, God is present, and present in the most intimate way: I can turn inward to find Him, and what I do, bolstered by that turn inward, will provide the answer to my prayer, such as it is. This view does not preclude, as I've said before, help from spiritual friends, guides, guardians, and teachers on the Other Side who might pick up my calls for help. But these spirits are far from omnipotent, and they cannot be faulted—as God can—for not "answering my prayer." Their power is limited to telepathic, mind-to-mind intrusions and can easily be ignored. I wonder if my prayers for Louie's good fortune—his career as a professor—received an assist from such a quarter, but I think it very unlikely that it was God, God in the fullest sense, God the Creator of the universe, who pulled it off. The best prayer, of course—and I think you will agree up to a point—is meditation on the God within, just being there with Him, in Him, as Him.

This Vedantic theology makes room for a new interpretation of the Nicene Creed. Jesus is not some unique, supernatural eruption of Godhead on the planet, but a prototype of what we all are. All of us have a divine nature in our depths, and all of us can freely embark on the process of accessing it and letting it take us to the destination we were all made for. Jesus did this to a degree perhaps unparalleled, but that was because he let himself be led by his divine nature to an unparalleled degree. But what he achieved we can too—though probably not in a single earth life—because our nature is the same as his.

Jesus, then, is our hero and our model. When we receive him in communion, we ritually act out our resolve to reach the same heights he achieved. We take into ourselves his resolve and his strength. He is not more divine than we are. What he achieved, we can too.

God's will for all of us is that we let our divine nature shine through more and more clearly—in our present life, in purgatorial spheres, in the higher heavens. As we progress, our bodies will thin out and cease to have the forms they now have. But they will always be bodies of one sort or another, and these bodies will always be material to one degree or another. If our souls ever shed this materiality altogether, we would cease to exist as individual selves. Our souls, being divine, would gravitate back to and merge with the Source. This would completely defeat God's purpose, which is to multiply the divine joy indefinitely and eternally. Non-Dualist Vedanta—and there are several schools of Vedanta—advocates the shedding of all bodies, however gross or subtle, and calls it freedom (moksha). It welcomes a complete merger with the Divine, as if every kind of individuality, however spiritualized, were a kind of holy egoism and should eventually be outgrown. This form of Vedanta I completely reject.

I asked above, "Now why would I choose Vedanta over Christianity?" Let me make two points in closing. First, now you see that I reject the final conclusion of Vedanta's most prominent school. Christianity's teaching of the "communion of saints" is dear to my heart. I have no desire to surrender the very thing so preciously cultivated across eons: my soul with its ever more rarified body. That would be, in my view, a suicide, an affront to God. Is such a thing possible? Theoretically yes, for the will is free at every level. Does such a thing ever happen? I don't know.

Second, I don't think my theology is un-Christian. I'm aware, of course, that most Christians would think it is and would condemn it. But I suspect Christ himself would not. All earth's theologies are primitive. How likely is it that 300 bishops gathered in Nicaea got it right for all time 1700 years ago? I think that you and I will see things much more clearly a few years after our deaths, and that we'll chuckle at our conceits. I look forward to our visits as we add up our earth errors and argue over whose dense brain happened to see things more clearly. We have provided each other a long and precious friendship rare for earth, and I look for it to continue in the realms beyond.

Stafford

*　*　*　*　*　*　*　*　*　*　*

July 16, 2012
Dear Stafford,

Many thanks for reading the Sokolowski essay. The objection you raise would be telling for a non-Trinitarian monotheism, for in such a setting God existing without a created world could not fully be love, since He would have no one other than Himself to love. He would be, as you say, impoverished, given the place of love in the life of persons. But the Trinitarian Christian God is a God of persons loving each other, a God whose entire life is interpersonal love. Such a God does not need a created world in order to exist as a God of love. When this God creates a world, the

Father creates it through the Son, so that the created persons in it are "sons in the Son," participants in the love that already exists in God. God does not become a lover by creating a world, but He draws a world into the already existing currents of divine love.

It seems to me that you do not do justice to what Christians believe about the interpersonal love that flows within the Trinity. It is as if you thought that this love could not be love in the same full sense in which God loves a creature. But consider that Christians believe that the Son is *generated* by the Father and *derives all of His being* from the Father. This is why Norris Clarke in one place describes the Son as "subsistent gratitude"–just because the Son has received everything from the Father. This is love that is analogous to the love of a child for its parents, and hence a real love. A real love that according to Christian belief existed in God before there was any created world.

Sokolowski's approach to the transcendence of the Christian God over the world seems to me to be extremely fruitful. Consider the contrast that he draws to *the pagan conceptions that keep God as part of the world—the best part indeed, but still part of it—and thus somehow in need of the world.* Sokolowski sees a freedom and generosity in the creative activity of God who does not need to create in order to be Himself. As for God's providence over the world, Sokolowski thinks that God by this transcendence is in a position, so to say, to exercise a detailed personal providence without constantly disrupting the laws of nature. A god existing in the world will have to compete with natural laws when he acts in nature.

I have in our exchange often said that God for you seems something less than the living God of Christianity, that your God seems to me to be a being that you assimilate too much to the finite world and its finite structures. I think I first made this objection to you when you seemed to say that God can't keep track of all His creatures at the same time, but has to move His attention away from some of them in order to turn it towards others of them. Your view of God's limited attention makes a certain sense if God is indeed in the world as one being among others, but it doesn't make sense, and indeed seems grossly anthropomorphic, if God transcends the world in the sense that He is fully God even without it and in the sense that He creates it and sustains it out of nothing.

One of the main ideas in your last message does indeed seem like a return to something we discussed earlier, and this is perhaps a sign of a certain circularity setting in, which may in turn indicate that we are nearing the end. I refer to your idea that each of us exists as a divine cell of God and is literally "one in being" with God. This is the very opposite of Christian creation: instead of being created out of nothing, you say that we are divine beings, "consubstantial" with God, indistinguishable from the God-man. Your view is even more opposed to Christian creation than is pagan theology. According to pagan theology, as interpreted by Sokolowski, we arise out of the world and are then subject to God, but we do not start "in God" in your sense. In the course of our exchange I repeatedly called this view of yours a species of pantheism, and I still think this is the right designation for it. (I realize that you are not a pantheist of the kind that favors a final dissolution of persons into God, but the "of one being with God" that you do favor makes for a pantheism all its own.)

You perhaps think that there is little difference between calling us divine cells of God or calling us beings created out of nothing by God. You may say that, after all, Christians believe that they are called to be "partakers" in the divine nature ("grant that by this mystery of water and wine we may become partakers of His divinity who was pleased to become partaker of our humanity"). You think that you can't differ from Christians all that much when you say that we all literally have the divine nature. The difference between being divine and partaking in the divine nature may seem slight. But the exact magnitude of this difference is one of the great issues of our exchange, for I have held, and you have denied, that the difference is huge. I have argued that we get one kind of religion if our divinization is set within our creaturehood, and that we get another and fundamentally different kind of religion if our divinization is understood to exclude Christian creaturehood. And I have argued that only the former view can be reasonably called Christian—the non-pantheistic view, the one according to which our divinization is in the order of grace and not of nature, and according to which we are "in Christ" but are not second Christs. I have wanted to reach agreement with you, not on the truth of the non-pantheist creation view—I never imagined I could convince you of that—but only on the fact that it is the only possible Christian view.

It often happens that a great deal turns on a small difference. Take one of the heavenly Mozart melodies, such as the adagio of the clarinet concerto; change a few notes and the heavenly melody is ruined. Speak of divine cells in God instead of creatures of God the creator, and you turn the Christian religion into something entirely different.

By the way, the problem of theodicy seems to me to become a far greater problem for you than it ever was for Christians. To the extent that human persons are bad, God is bad, on your account, since they are one in being with God. If some human beings are irreversibly bad, then part of God is irreversibly bad, since they are parts of God. For Christians the problem of theodicy arises from the evil in the world; for you the problem arises from the evil existing in God himself.

One more thought on this vexed question of receiving communion. I'm not trying to convince you of the Catholic understanding of it, and so it is not really to the point when you lay out your non-Catholic understanding of it. My point of concern has to do with respect for the views of others. When Pope Benedict took his shoes off on entering the mosque in Istanbul he did it, not as required by divine law, but as required by human consideration. It is this kind of respect that I think should keep you away from communion, at least in Catholic churches. Otherwise you are like a visitor to a mosque who insists on tramping around with his shoes on, and who, when censured for his behavior, answers that God couldn't possibly care whether we wear shoes or not.

If you want to gather with like-minded friends to break bread and remember Jesus, no Catholic could possibly have any objection, though we would regret that you don't have a "higher" view of the eucharistic celebration. You give offense not by having your way of breaking bread in Jesus' name but by "crashing" the Catholic ceremony of breaking the eucharistic bread, and by trying to impose on it a foreign meaning.

Thus there is here not only the issue of respecting the religious views of others, but also, in my opinion, an issue of truthfulness and integrity. I can't help seeing a defect of truthfulness in someone with your views who tries to impose on the Catholic rite a foreign meaning. It would be more truthful for you to have your eucharistic commemoration apart from the Catholic rite.

I see a similar defect in truthfulness when you propose a new Vedantic interpretation of the Nicene Creed, according to which everyone has the divine nature in the same way that the Son of God has it. You seem to me to be like Henry Higgins when he sings, "why can't a woman be more like a man?" You express the same mindset of abolishing fundamental differences when you say, "why can't the Nicene Creed be more like a Vedantic text?" Men and women are irreducibly different, and the religion that is centered on one God-man is irreducibly different from the religion that makes a God-man out of all of us. The religion in which the one God-man redeems us is irreducibly different from the religion in which we redeem ourselves by living out of our divine nature. I understand why you feel, as you say, uncomfortable in reciting the Nicene Creed: the work of re-interpretation that you are attempting doesn't work, doesn't make sense. You would be far more true to yourself if you were to let the creed go: you don't believe it, so don't recite it. It would be more truthful to pray something in place of it that you do believe, just as it would be more truthful to remember the last supper in some form that is outside of the Catholic sacrament.

You are right that there is something remarkable about Newman's views on non-Christian religions. He received from the Greek fathers views that generously acknowledge the presence of God in these religions. Following them he speaks of "the dispensation of paganism." He cites with sympathy the opinion of St. Clement of Alexandria that the coming of Christ was prepared in the providence of God not only by the Hebrew prophets but also by the Greek philosophers. And yet Newman relates all of the grace and truth in pagan religions back to Christ, as when in the same passage from which you quote he also says, discussing Job, who is presented in scripture as a pagan: "Why should not the book of Job be accepted by us, as a gracious intimation given us, who are God's sons, for our comfort, when we are anxious about our brethren who are still 'scattered abroad' in an evil world; an intimation that *the Sacrifice, which is the hope of Christians, has its power and its success, wherever men seek God with their whole heart?*" (my italics). In other words, the "pluralist" position of people like Paul Knitter is entirely foreign to Newman.

I can imagine you saying, after reading this, "why is John always driving a wedge between us when there is so much that we share in religion?" As I have said before, I don't feel quite "safe" in exploring our common ground as long as important things are being run together that are really different. I feel that I am somehow acquiescing in the fatal conflation of fundamentally different things. But if we can speak with a yes that is yes and a no that is no, if we can let each thing be itself and not blend it into some other thing, then the condition is fulfilled for such sharing—real and significant sharing—as is still possible between us.

Could this be the natural conclusion of our exchange, at least for now?

In friendship,
John

* * * * * * * * * * *

July 30, 2012
Dear John,

Your last letter is a good roundup of your position. But halfway through you said something quite unexpected, something quite new. In addressing it my position will become clearer, both to you and to myself. Here is what you wrote:

"By the way, the problem of theodicy seems to me to become a far greater problem for you than it ever was for Christians. To the extent that human persons are bad, God is bad, on your account, since they are one in being with God. If some human beings are irreversibly bad, then part of God is irreversibly bad, since they are parts of God. For Christians the problem of theodicy arises from the evil in the world; for you the problem arises from the evil existing in God himself."

This is the very challenge I throw at my Non-Dualist Vedanta friends, who claim that our true self is none other than Brahman (the Hindu version of ultimate reality), who is eternal perfection in every sense. It's long been my belief that their defense of Brahman's freedom from suffering and sin is unintelligible and self- contradictory if He/It is our true self, which is obviously implicated in every kind of sin and suffering. So how is my defense different from theirs?

They hold that there is no difference whatever between the deepest layer of the human self (Atman) and Brahman, and that the states of transcendental bliss arrived at in the deepest meditative states are proof of non-difference. My own view is that these world-class meditators (for whom I have great respect) have squarely centered their consciousness in their souls' depths and that it's not surprising they found bliss. For their souls do come from God and share in his substance. They are like drops of spray flung out of the ocean. If you taste the drop, it will have a salty taste, just like the ocean. But the drop is not the ocean.

So God, in my view, is not bad just because some or all of us are.

God and we share the following: consciousness, free will, and an environment. This is significant, this is to say a lot. But God's consciousness is supremely comprehensive whereas ours is narrow and blinkered. And whereas God uses his free will to optimize goodness and beauty in his universe, we too often use ours to optimize what we, in our ignorance, take to be good *for us,* while ignoring the general good. And while God resides in the highest heaven, amidst beauty and goodness indescribable, we fight for happiness in a difficult environment in a body condemned to death. So it makes sense that we would be fallible, ignorant, weak creatures in spite of our divine pedigree.

Have I accounted for our soul's capacity for sin while still being formed of the divine substance? I think my account is intelligible, though obviously speculative—but no more speculative than what has come down through the ages as Christian orthodoxy. And, for me, more plausible.

Regarding my participation in the eucharist as a party-crasher, if there were not people like me, nothing would ever change. Sometimes the envelope needs to be pushed. It doesn't get pushed if critics of the status quo simply exit the building. For most Catholics the Church is not perfect; it hasn't gotten everything figured out; the rules have changed in the past and will change again in the future. And they should.

Jesus had the heart of a reformer, and so do I. He created a lot more havoc in the temple in Jerusalem than I do by taking communion with secretly held unorthodox opinions about what I am doing. I don't like giving offense, and, to my knowledge, I don't. Nevertheless, I do feel more at home in an Anglican church than a Catholic. As the local priest says, "All are welcome at Christ's table." I think that's the way Jesus would have wanted it.

Harvard University's Diana Eck wrote a brilliant, much celebrated book, *Encountering God,* that I wish I could share with you. She is a Methodist Christian by birth and upbringing, and a Hinduized Christian today. The change happened because she lived among Hindus, several of them saints, as a graduate student. I can think of no better way to truly understand me than by reading that book. Otherwise you'll continue to think that something unfortunate happened to me when I began to stray from the religion of my birth. I wish you didn't have to live with this disquiet.

Stafford

*   *   *   *   *   *   *   *   *   *   *

August 14, 2012
Dear Stafford,

I know you don't want me to leave your last message without a response.

There must be something I am missing in your defense of your Vedantic position. It seems to me that you make it understandable how we go wrong (because of ignorance, limited perspective, bodiliness, etc.) but don't make it understandable how the wrong we do is not wrong done by God and does not compromise the goodness of God. Let me say it like this. You seem to think of each of us as being divine in the way in which Christians believe that the Son of God is divine—begotten not made, consubstantial with the Father. Instead of God having one divine Son, all of us, you say, are divine sons and daughters. We are not adoptive sons and daughters but have a "filiation" exactly like that of the Son of God. Well, just as Jesus Christ, if he had done wrong, would have made God to that extent a wrongdoer, so all of our wrongdoing infects God, on your view of who we are, with wrong. But all of this trouble with theodicy vanishes once you let us human beings exist as creatures and not as divine beings.

As for receiving Catholic communion, let me try this approach. In order to agitate meaningfully for change in Catholic sacramental practice, you need to be "of the household of faith," as St. Paul says. Otherwise you are like the Westerner who keeps his shoes on in mosques as a protest against the Moslem practice. He may think of himself as the cutting edge of much-needed change, as one who bravely pushes the envelope, but he is in reality quite absurdly imposing foreign standards on the incommensurable religious world of Islam. He should go to worship in places where shoes are worn, and should leave the mosques to the Moslems. Otherwise he is guilty of a certain religious intolerance, or religious imperialism. He isn't closely enough linked with Moslem belief to have a right to modify Moslem practice in mosques. In a somewhat similar way, it seems to me that you, for all your points of contact with Catholic belief, have rejected so many fundamentals of the faith that you are a kind of outsider with respect to what we Catholics believe about the body and blood of the Lord, and that it is therefore not appropriate for you to agitate to change the terms of the eucharistic celebration.

Notice that this issue of participating in the eucharist mirrors our issue of what is Christian and what is non-Christian: in both cases you are blending where I am dividing; you are saying that apparently opposed things are really the same, where I am saying that each thing is itself and is not another. Hence the issue of sacramental practice is really a fundamental part of our exchange—more so than I had first thought.

I have requested the book by Diana Eck from another library; I am eager to read it, most of all as a way of understanding you better.

After so many words and arguments, let's not fail to go to prayer, and to remember each other before the Lord.

Your devoted friend,
John

P.S. I just noticed that I neglected to respond to an important point you raised in your letter of February 26, 2012, where you say you can't make good sense of the Christian idea of "substitutionary atonement." You say that you can make sense of the passion of Christ as an expression of His solidarity with us in our suffering, but cannot make sense of His passion having any real efficacy in delivering us from sin and evil. Go back for a minute to Newman's harrowing description of the fallenness of the human condition that I quoted in an earlier letter. You may recall that he speaks of "some terrible aboriginal calamity" in which the human race must be implicated. The Christian idea of atonement, as I understand it, is built on the idea that we human beings do not have, in our own resources, what it takes to undo this calamity. Only a divine initiative, breaking into our calamitous condition from without, can deliver us. Just as it is Pelagianism, as I argued earlier, to think that I can work out my salvation on my own, so it would be Pelagianism all over again to think that the human race can work its way out of its radical fallenness on its own. We need a redeemer who can bear the burden that crushes us. The words of the prophet Isaiah speak of just such a redeemer: "He was pierced for our offenses, crushed for our sins; on him is the chastisement that makes us whole; by his stripes we are healed." So you see that my acceptance of Christian atonement is of one piece with my rejection of Pelagian self-salvation.

Stafford's Afterword

Perhaps a better title for this book would have been *Two Ways of Being Christian*. John has made it clear to me that I do not fit into the Catholic Church as it is presently structured. But what about Christianity? We all know that there are many ways to be Christian, John included. John, however, does not think I fit into any of those ways. I see it differently. For me the core of Christianity—and of Judaism too, incidentally—is the Two Great Commandments. In Jesus' words, "You must love the Lord your God with all your heart, with all your soul, and with all your mind. This is the greatest and the first commandment. The second resembles it: You must love your neighbor as yourself. On these two commandments hang the whole Law, and the Prophets also" (Matt 22: 37-40). Jesus elsewhere elaborates on the second in his encounter with the rich young man. When the man asks Jesus what he must do to possess eternal life, Jesus answers that he must keep the commandments: "You must not kill. You must not commit adultery. You must not steal. You must not bring false witness. Honor you father and mother, and: you must love your neighbor as yourself" (Matt 19: 18-19). If the young man had been willing to take the next step, sell all he had and give it to the poor, Jesus would have embraced him as the newest apostle. Would he have embraced me with my set of beliefs? I think so, for it wasn't beliefs that impressed Jesus. What impressed him was how well one committed oneself to the practice of the Two Great Commandments.

I consider myself a "Great Commandments Christian"—a follower of Jesus' most essential teaching. John thinks this is important but not nearly enough. For him there are the great Church councils, especially the Council of Nicaea, which in 325 A.D. defined Jesus' relation to the Father as co-eternal and coequal God. The Nicene Creed became the litmus test of Catholic Christianity from that point on. If you didn't accept its declarations, you were a heretic. John is a Nicene Christian.

I have no objections to this kind of Christianity in the case of my dear friend John. It anchors him in a faith that has brought forth great personal holiness. But the Nicene claim has brought enormous suffering into the world, as error always does in the long run. Islam sees Catholicism's claim that Jesus is God's equal as damnable, for it is the ultimate insult to Allah to erect any man, however great, as God's equal "partner." This teaching enflames the Muslim and teaches him contempt for Christianity. We are watching the fallout in today's world.

In my capacity as a professor of the world's religions, I have come into personal contact with living saints who have been nurtured by their various religions. I have been especially impressed by the great holiness in several Hindus and Buddhists I've met. Nothing could be clearer to me than that there are other ways to salvation besides Christianity. Yet I am deeply attracted to Jesus' religion and am tempted to claim for it first place among the world's religions in spite of the errors that grew up around it long after his death. I am attracted to Jesus' emphasis on love and forgiveness. His great Sermon on the Mount (Matt 5-7) is a call to heroic action unlike anything in the world's other scriptures. And his estimate of human evil, its enormity and destructiveness, reveals a realism that the world desperately needs to heed.

I attend an Anglican church to come into contact with the evil in me and to get help in ferreting it out. I've learned to tolerate the Creed rather well, for I understand it as a statement that grew out of a love for Jesus so intense that it billowed out into full divinization. On Sunday mornings I recite the Creed, wincing at the literal claims, but remembering their holy source and quietly interpreting it in my own way. As for communion, I receive it because I think Jesus would be happy to have me sit at his table if he were presiding. As for my fellow parishioners, all of whom are more traditional than I, I don't trouble them with my eccentricities. They know I am different, but they expect me to be. We enjoy each other; it's good to be around people who love God and do their best to love each other.

I want to thank John for the opportunity to debate him in our exchange of letters—which, incidentally, was never intended to turn into a book when we started out. His concern for me grows out of a friendship that goes back to our late teen years, when we used to get together and play chess, or talk about our girlfriends (for which we usually required considerable solace), or examine the teachings of the Church we loved equally, and that we had earlier served as little altar boys during Mass at Jesuit Spring Hill College.

I fully expect, as I said in one of the letters above, to compare notes with him when we have cleared the Great Divide. If Nicaea's teachings have currency over there, I would be immensely surprised. The Franciscan spiritual master Richard Rohr tells us why: "To deny change and growth is to deny the obvious, yet humans seem good at that. The ride is the destination, and the goal is never clearly in sight. To stay on the ride, to trust the trajectory, to know it is moving, and moving somewhere always better, is just about the best way to describe religious faith."

As a boy I must have recited the Apostles' Creed a thousand times. Many of you know it well. Here is the way I would say it today. Perhaps it will serve as a better litmus test than the Nicene Creed for determining whether I am a Christian, or perhaps even whether you are—for I know I am not alone.

I believe in God the Father and Mother, creator of the universe. I believe in the teachings of Jesus Christ, whose life was tragically cut short by corrupt men he outspokenly condemned. He was crucified like a criminal under Pontius Pilate, but his spirit did not die. Shortly after his death his closest friends saw him in spirit and took heart that he was, while in heaven, still with them; and they could not contain their joy; and out of that joy grew a young movement that would soon be labeled Christianity. I believe that the same divine spirit in Jesus is in all of us and that the Christian Church exists to help us grow into saints modeled after him. I believe that we are called to forgive and love each other and that we will be forgiven and loved in turn. I believe that life is everlasting and heaven is the ultimate destination for which all men and women were created. Amen.

John's Afterword

I thank Stafford for entering in to this dialogue with me. We now understand each other better than we ever did before. We have challenged each other to go deeper. I rejoice to see how many elements of religion we still share. Our friendship has grown through our exchange.

But we are still at odds on some fundamentals of faith. Throughout our exchange I have been pushing back against Stafford's claim to believe like a Christian. It is only natural that, in his final word, he would re-assert this claim. And he reasserts it by saying that his Christianity centers around the two great commandments, love of God and love of neighbor. My Christianity, by contrast, he says, centers around a doctrine affirmed at the Council of Nicea in 325, namely the divinity of Christ. Stafford concludes that he may not be a Christian in my narrow sense, but that he certainly counts as one in his more abundant sense of Christianity. This final word of Stafford's merits a response, which will be my final word in our exchange.

We do not want to lose ourselves in mere verbal disputes, so let me grant without further discussion that Stafford describes in his Afterword a broad and loose sense of "Christian" according to which he is a Christian. In this sense many Hindu swamis and Buddhist monks are also Christians. In my exchange with Stafford I have above all wanted to say that Catholic Christianity is something all its own and something entirely different from Christianity broadly and loosely conceived. Stafford seems to think that in moving from Catholic to "Christian" he has made a relatively minor adjustment to his Catholicism. I have argued that this is not a minor adjustment but a move into a different kind of religion altogether. This is the issue between us: how big is the gap between his broad, pluralistically conceived "Christianity" and Catholic Christianity? I repeat that the issue is not exactly whether Catholic Christianity is true, but whether it can be understood in the pluralist manner of John Hick without being fundamentally misunderstood.

Now in his Afterword Stafford suggests that we have been debating the Christological doctrines that were declared at the Council of Nicea in 325. But this greatly understates the scope of our debate; what is at issue is the collision of two fundamentally different kinds of religion. Thus if you hold with Stafford that God generates human beings out of His own substance, as the Father generates the Son, so that man exists as ontologically divine, then you have one kind of religion; but if you hold with Catholic Christianity that God creates man *ex nihilo*, so that each human being exists through God as a creature of God, you have an entirely different kind of religion. If you hold with Stafford that an individual human being arises when a part of God's being is contracted by matter into an individual, you have one sense of who we are as individuals; but if you hold with Christianity that such an extrinsic principle of individuation can never do justice to the incommunicable selfhood of a human person, and if you hold that only an intrinsic principle of individuation can escape the charge of pantheism, you have an entirely different conception of who we are as individual persons. It is the same with holding that God's nature is material and that He occupies space; Catholic Christians will say that God is thereby installed in the finite world and no longer exists as the infinite, world-transcendent creator-God whom we encounter in Christian revelation. Again: Stafford owns up to being a kind of Pelagian who believes in self-salvation; fundamentally opposed to this is the Christian teaching of the element of "gratuity and election" in God's initiative towards those whom He saves. Stafford says that God is always available to us whenever we turn to Him, just like any other object of knowledge is available to us; but Christianity teaches that our knowledge of God depends not only on our turning to Him but most of all on His inscrutable self-disclosure to us. In other words, in Stafford's religion revelation plays no role, whereas it is fundamental to Catholic Christianity. Again: Stafford implies that God and the world form an indivisible whole; Christianity says that God could have been all there is.

Thus to say that I propose a Nicene litmus-test for being a Christian, does not do justice to all that I really said. My profession of Christ as God-man is embedded in fundamental affirmations about the nature of God, of matter, of personhood, of interpersonal encounter, and it was these surrounding affirmations that have stood at the center of our debate. I was intrigued by the difference between the human person as he appears within the Christian theology of creation, and as he appears apart from it. I wanted to share with Stafford what I take to be the great fruitfulness of Christian personalism. If in these letters I doubt that his religious position counts as Christian, this is not just because he rejects a particular Christian doctrine, but because the entire God-creature relation in his religious thought seems to me to be at odds with what Catholic Christians believe.

In addition to all of these non-Christological issues about God and man, Stafford and I of course also collided over the divinity of Christ. Before finishing I have to say a word about his treatment of that teaching in his Afterword.

Stafford belittles this Nicene doctrine on the grounds that, as he says, it is only a "belief" and that Jesus was not concerned with what we believe. Thus the welcome that Stafford expects from Jesus is entirely independent of Stafford's religious beliefs. But is this not a glib and oversimple account of what Jesus looks for in a disciple? How will Stafford explain why Jesus asked the disciples, "who do people say the Son of Man is" and "who do you say the Son of Man is"? Why does Jesus praise Peter for confessing that Jesus is "the Christ, the Son of the Living God," if beliefs count for nothing for Jesus? Why does Jesus call attention to the supernatural source of Peter's profession ("my father in heaven"), if this belief is not supremely important? Why does Jesus invest Peter with the keys of the kingdom of heaven on the basis of Peter's confession, if the truth of his confession is not supremely important? If Stafford had been present and had disagreed with Peter, and had said to Jesus, "No, you are not the Son of the Living God, you are just one of the prophets come back to life," would Jesus not have rebuked Stafford? And why? Because Stafford would have professed a false belief about Jesus. For Jesus it was all-important that his disciples receive truly the self-disclosure that He gives of Himself. He never plays off the two great commandments against knowing who He really is, as Stafford seems to do.

Let me conclude by returning to the religious first principles that have been my primary concern throughout this exchange. One last time I want to call attention to a certain pattern of thought that I discern in Stafford. On the one hand, Stafford tends to divinize each human being, as when he conceives of each human being as a "part" of God, or when he claims for each of us the same relation to the Father that the Son possesses. But on the other hand he "finitizes" God, as when he thinks of Him as a material being, or when he thinks of Him as being capable of doing evil, or being surprised at the human persons who arise in His world. This "closing the space" between God and the creature is my main reason for saying that Stafford's religious position is at a great remove from the Christian position.

Alas, I remain to the end in the unenviable position of contesting Stafford's attempts to identify as a Christian. I must seem to some readers like a sullen and unwelcoming person. But Kierkegaard used to say that he had the calling to make Christianity more difficult for his Danish contemporaries, and perhaps I have this same calling in relation to Stafford.

The case of Kierkegaard is instructive. Many educated people in Denmark and Germany thought that Hegel's philosophy faithfully expressed Christianity; Kierkegaard protested, saying that being a Christian was something altogether different from, and immeasurably more difficult than, being a follower of Hegel. Of course, Stafford is no Hegelian. But there is this parallel: just as Kierkegaard refused to reduce Christianity to Hegelianism, so I have to refuse to reduce Christianity to Stafford's pluralist theology. Just as Kierkegaard saw in "Hegelian Christianity" the worst kind of syncretism, so I see in Stafford's "Vedantic Christianity" something similarly syncretist. Perhaps in our age too we need to hear prophetic voices like those of Kierkegaard and Newman admonishing us to see Christianity for what it is and not to blend it with what it is not.